Not-for-Profit (5th) Edition

Welcome to an educational and entertaining encounter with your RV's "unique" appliances. This *Primer* was explicitly designed to get all RVers thinking in a *different* direction.

Written for all RV enthusiasts, especially those who are:
- Initially "CONSIDERING" RVing,
- Just "BEGINNING" their RVing experience,
- Have been "CAMPING for YEARS," or,
- Living the dream of "FULL-TIMING."

The information within will clearly demonstrate that an RV "house" battery is NOT the same as a car "starting" battery. Nor do they function alike. It will also help everyone understand just how many different "things" in their RV are actually powered by 12-Volts, as well as why this system is considered to be the RV's "lifeblood."

This Primer endeavors to help all readers establish a practical awareness of "basic" 12-Volt, RV Electricity. Principally, a knowledge level that will enable each reader to start thinking in terms of efficient "use and maintenance" of their 12-Volt system, and, thus, preventing the proverbially frustrating, "I THINK THE BATTERIES ARE DEAD?!"

The included Editorial *Comments* are based on the author's sixty years of experience using and living in RVs (including more than a decade of recent "full-time" RVing) and conducting the business of repairing RVs. Now, he is concentrating on educating the RV owners.

Also included are lots of "tips and tricks" on how to help your RV's battery bank work more efficiently and "live" longer.

The ladies are especially encouraged to read everything between this book's covers. Then they will understand why it is more probable to check for a "blown fuse" rather than a "tripped circuit breaker."

Why a "Not-for-Profit" Edition?

When it was first written, this *Primer* was an integral part of the author's **Understanding Your RV** series of four books for all RVers. Unfortunately, it has been out of circulation for far too long and was not available for several editions as a stand-alone book. It was, however, offered as a free "bonus" book when purchasing the other three primer books ("Shore Power," "Appliances," and "Holding Tanks") as a set.

Ideally, as a publishing company, we would like to make up for many readers' angst because of its stand-alone scarcity and give the book away for free. Regrettably, to do so has proven to be very challenging. There are several "production" layers in a publication venture, which require financial compensation.

As a result, we are offering this updated (5th) edition of the "Battery Power" *Primer* to our readers for the cost of minimal fees — those required by others who are a part of the "production" process: Professional Preparation Fees, Printing Fees, Promotion Fees, and Sales Processing Fees, to name just a few.

It is appropriately referred to as a "Not-for-Profit" book because the author, while retaining his copyrights, is foregoing Royalty income from the sale of this special edition of "Battery Power." Also, this *Primer* will <u>not</u> be available for what is known as "Expanded Distribution," meaning it will not be available for Volume Wholesale Purchasing. Hence the "Not Eligible for Wholesale Purchase" tag at the bottom of the pages.

Understanding Your RV's "BATTERY POWER"

12-Volt Electricity

- - A Primer - -

by

Dale Lee Sumner

Retired Master Certified RV Service Technician

Not-Eligible-for-Wholesale-Purchase

Not-for-Profit (5th) Edition
Copyright © 2020 by Dale Lee Sumner

All rights reserved. No part of this book may be reproduced or transmitted in any form by any means, electronic or mechanical, including photocopying and recording, or by any information storage and retrieval system, without permission in writing from the publisher, except in the case of brief quotations embodied in critical reviews or articles.

Published by SUMDALUS-USA
sales.sumdalus-usa@outlook.com

Printed in the United States of America
ISBN: 978-0-9974634-9-1

Cover Image – by Author

<u>Other Published RV "**Primer**" books available from www.sumdalus.com</u>

Understanding Your RV's "SHORE POWER"
120 Volt Electricity

Understanding Your RV's "APPLIANCES"
Refrigerator, Furnace, Water Heater, and Rooftop Air Conditioner

Understanding Your RV's "HOLDING TANKS"
Bio-Waste Management

My RV "LOGBOOK"
A Vital Record of My RV's Equipment & Appliance Information

Dedicated to

My Wife.

She is:

My Love,

My Partner,

and

My Lifeblood!

ACKNOWLEDGMENT

I continue to be especially thankful to Mr. Ed Sweetman, the director and exceptional instructor at the RV Tech School I attended many years ago. His depth of knowledge about RVs, his unfailing encouragement, and his willingness to be available to answer any question or to help solve an unusual problem have always been significant assets to me through the years. Thank you so much, Ed!!

DISCLAIMER

The text, photos, diagrams, and analogies within this book are meant to guide the reader toward a better understanding of the 12 VDC electrical system associated with a Recreational Vehicle (RV). They may not be complete, may contain minor errors, and may not apply accurately to an owner's specific problem. They are not to be relied upon as guidance for repairing anyone's RV's 12-Volt electrical systems or components. Each RV owner is responsible for any hazards she/he (s/he) encounter or produce if they work on their RV's electrical system. The legal right to work on some parts of your system may be limited in your state. Contacting a local RV dealership to schedule a "bring it in" appointment or contacting a local, independent RV service technician to "come to" an RV site are always options. Either one may be required to accomplish necessary repairs.

NOTE

Most photographs, images, diagrams, or charts not sourced/credited within this Primer were designed and/or produced by the author. The publisher has made every reasonable effort to contact all copyright holders. Any errors which may have occurred are inadvertent. Anyone who, for any reason, has not been contacted is invited to communicate with the publisher so that a full acknowledgment may be made in subsequent editions of this work.

INTRODUCTION

Webster's dictionary defines a *Primer* (prĭm´ər – rhymes with 'trimmer') as "a small book covering the fundamentals of a topic."

This "small book" concentrates on the 12-Volt Electrical (a.k.a. Battery Power) System in your RV. It was not designed to be a high-level, scientifically correct, know-all, or end-all document to satisfy the most critical of electrical engineers. (In their own right, they are operating at a different level of expertise than the rest of us.) Instead, it was written to provide the typical RVer (*J.* [Jane or John] *Q. **Public***) with a baseline of understanding about the 12-Volt Electrical System that controls most of the equipments/appliances inside their RV.

During my 12-Volt Electricity seminar, I conveyed to attending RVers that "lifeblood" is defined as a "vital or life-giving force or compo-nent, and the 12-Volt Electrical System is, without question, the very lifeblood of their RV." To such a statement, I often receive somewhat skeptically raised eyebrows and a number of upheld hands demanding attention. I am so frequently challenged about this; I would even bet that if I asked twelve different RVers, "What do you think is the 'lifeblood' of your RV?" I would receive a dozen different answers.

Hmm. Right now, you are probably wondering why I would make such a bold statement about the 12-Volt Electrical System. Well, this book is designed to explain the "why."

Throughout my years as an RV Service Technician, I found that most RVers don't even have a rudimentary understanding of batteries. Their only previous experience with large batteries (bigger than flashlight batteries) has been limited to the battery in their car. Basically, "When I turn the key, it starts the car," and, "It either works, or it doesn't." And usually, "*Aw, Shucks!*" (or something like that) when it doesn't.

The "LIFEBLOOD" of your RV

Unfortunately, while the 12-Volt Electrical System is the single largest system in any RV, it is, without a doubt, the least understood, most frequently ignored, and repeatedly abused system in any RV. Sure, most RVers realize there is a battery (or several batteries – referred to as a "bank") in their unit. Still, very few realize their importance, how they work, or how to properly care for them.

Did you know the lights in your RV constitute the principal "appliance" that consumes more 12-Volt (battery) power than any other? That's because, in the vast majority of RVs, all the lights are powered by 12-Volts, even the fluorescent ones. (**Comment:** There are only a few RVs that have one or two lights powered by 120 Volt [shore] power, and they are predictably located in a room slide-out in a travel trailer or 5th wheel. [And we're not talking about the lamps you brought into the RV.] **Another Comment:** Your mother's reminder about turning off the lights when you leave a room really holds true in an RV – especially if you are dry camping [a.k.a. boondocking].)

Besides providing power for the lights in the RV, the battery bank also provides power for a very critical safety device – The LP alarm! This alarm is hard-wired (directly connected) to the "house" battery 100% of the time. There is no "ON/OFF" switch for this alarm! (**Comment:** A Carbon Monoxide [CO] Alarm is rarely hardwired to the battery. CO and Smoke/Fire alarms are usually powered by replaceable dry cell [flashlight type] batteries.)

Sidebar: The LP alarm, secondarily, functions as a low battery alarm. When the battery voltage is too low to power the LP alarm adequately, the alarm prudently uses the last bit of available battery power to let you know about the low power condition. Usually, at about 10.5 volts of battery power, it "chirps" (about once a minute) repeatedly to get your attention. You should make sure you know what your actual LP alarm sounds like by pressing the test button as prescribed by the manufacturer – optimally once a week. "Once a week!?" Oh, you think that's a lot. Frankly, it isn't a lot when you recognize the purpose of the alarm is to save your life. Consider the fact that most of the time you are in your RV, you are probably asleep. And I guarantee it's no fun to wake up dead because the alarm didn't function properly when an LP gas leak occurred So, TEST IT! Protect yourself and your loved ones.

(**Comment:** Most manufacturers of LP, CO, and Smoke alarms for RVs recommend replacing these alarms every five [5] years. All alarm sensing devices desensitize ["wears out"] over time. How old are your alarms? **Important:** Only install LP, CO, and/or Smoke alarms UL listed for Recreational Vehicle Use. The alarms you can get at the local hardware store probably aren't!!)

The battery bank is also called upon to provide power to many of our appliances and equipment within the RV. Typically, when I receive a trouble call from a prospective or previous customer, I hear comments such as:

"My lights are very dim."

"My furnace won't run at all."

"My refrigerator isn't running."

"My water heater won't run on LP."

"My air conditioner won't work."

Or, not surprisingly, "My LP alarm is chirping."

Hmm... Each of these customer comments automatically starts me thinking in terms of low 12-Volt power - - -

The lights aren't bright because of "low" 12-Volt power.

The furnace functions (fan motor and ignition board) operate totally on 12-Volt power.

You can set a refrigerator on AUTO or AC (both modes use 120 Volt generator power or shore power). Still, <u>a 12-Volt circuit board controls all of the refrigerator's functions</u>.

To work in LP mode, the water heater uses 12-Volt power to open the gas valve and initiate the igniter board operation.

Although the air conditioner is a 120 Volt appliance, it is controlled by a 12-Volt circuit board.

And, as you've already read, the LP alarm "chirps" when the 12-Volt power is too low.

(For in-depth explanations about how 12-Volts control 120-Volt appliances, please read the **Primer** titled, *Understanding Your RV's "APPLIANCES."* It also explains how the 12-Volt igniter boards work.)

So, the first question I always ask is, "When was the last time you added water to your battery/ies?"

I couldn't possibly count how many times I've received the response (after a long pause), "What does that have to do with anything?"

"I'll be there in about fifteen minutes," is my only reply.

Okay, reader, when was the last time you added water to your battery/ies? And, yes, "What that has to do with anything" will also be answered in detail in this *Primer*. There will even be important information provided about other facets of the RV 12-Volt Electrical System. I sincerely hope, when you are finished reading this book, you can honestly say, "Wow, I learned something!" or better still, "Now... it makes sense!"

Well, now, let's get started learning about

12-Volt RV Electricity

. . .

BASIC BATTERY FACTS

We're going to start things off with a somewhat perplexing statement.

As "phred" Tinseth (www.phrannie.org) was fond of saying, **"A 12-Volt Battery is NOT a 12-Volt Battery!"** He contended the term "12-Volt Battery" was just a "general" expression used to identify one specific "size" of battery – as opposed to a six-volt battery (which really isn't a six-volt battery, either). (**Comment:** I equate this concept to using the term "car" to refer to an *automobile* – which may actually be a 2-door or 4-door sedan, a convertible, a van, or even an SUV – so…what we call it "generically," isn't really what it is.)

Confused? Well, maybe this simple physics truth will help:

A fully-charged 12-Volt Battery, allowed to "rest" for several hours without anything attached to it (that means no load being drawn from it or charge going to it – in other words, disconnected electrically from the RV [a.k.a. an "Open-Circuit"]), will arrive at what is referred to as a "Charge Equilibrium." Using a digital voltmeter to test it, this charge equilibrium will measure somewhere between 12.60 to 12.69 Volts of Direct Current (VDC) across the terminals. So, in reality, a 12-Volt Battery is actually a "twelve point six something" volt battery. I guess it makes life a lot easier if we just call it a plain 'ole "12-Volt Battery!"

Let's add a little more confusion. Take a close look at this table.

Disconnected Battery Voltage (12V / 6V)	Approximate Charge Level
12.66 / 6.33	100%
12.51 / 6.25	80%
12.35 / 6.17	60%
12.19 / 6.09	40%
12.04 / 6.02	20%
11.81 / 5.91	0%

Naturally, when a telephoning customer tells me that s/he tested the battery and the voltage is "12-Volts," I can't help but wonder if the customer thought the values to the right of the decimal were unimportant and unintentionally rounded off the voltage, or if the battery s/he tested really is 80% discharged (or 20% charged).

Ladies and gentlemen, an actual reading of 12.04 volts is essentially a DEAD battery! There is not enough stored electricity left in the battery to effectively do anything for you. Please realize there are only about $85/100^{ths}$ of a volt representing the full charge range on a 12-Volt Battery. (12.66v – 11.81v = 0.85v).

WOW! It seems like this subject is becoming seriously complicated, so why don't we back up a little and look at a few battery basics. Let's first describe how they are put together; then, maybe, we'll find it easier to understand how they work.

To begin with, a battery is simply a repository of certain chemicals that, when allowed to react under controlled conditions, provide an electrical charge. Thus, the "capacity" of the battery is simply a measure of how much "charge" it can provide.

A really great **analogy** to explain the basics of a battery's charge, current, and voltage was written by Graham Legg, an electronics/electrical engineer with 25 years of experience, primarily designing battery charging systems. (*grahamlegg.talktalk.net/batts.html*)

> "Consider 'charge' to be the amount of water in a bucket (the battery). If that water starts to flow out, the speed at which it flows is called the 'current.' The greater the speed (the larger the current), the quicker the bucket is empty (battery drained/dead). The force driving the current is the water pressure – this is 'voltage' in electrical terms. All other things being equal, a higher pressure will cause the flow to be larger (a higher voltage will cause a greater current). If the water flows out of a hole in the bottom of the bucket, the bigger the hole, the less pressure it takes to drive out a given flow. The size of the hole is a measure of its resistance to the flow –

again, this is analogous to electrical resistance. A bucket of water emptying through a hole is similar to a battery discharging into a 'load' (anything the battery supplies current to, e.g., a fan, water pump, lights). As the water level drops, the pressure falls, and the current slows. The bigger the hole, the higher the pressure, the quicker this happens. Likewise, as a battery discharges, the voltage drops, and the current slows, until eventually, there is no voltage and no current. The higher the voltage, the greater the current, the quicker this happens."

Practically all batteries initially provided with our RVs are Lead-Acid type batteries. The Lead-Acid Battery that we know today was developed commercially in 1859 (Over 160 years ago!) by a French physicist named Gaston Planté. Functional batteries of a different type were actually discovered in the ruins of ancient Egypt and Babylon. So, undoubtedly, we can safely say that batteries have been around for a long, long time.

A **Lead-Acid Battery** is also called a "flooded" battery and sometimes called a "wet" battery. The flooding (or wetness) derives from the addition of an electrolyte (i.e., an acid that is a good ionic conductor but is not electronically conductive, as this would cause internal short-circuiting). Each cell in our RV battery is filled with Sulfuric Acid ($H_2SO_4[aq]$). The (aq) means that it is mixed with water and is not a "full strength" acid (actually 35% sulfuric acid and 65% water).

WARNING: Acid, no matter what the strength, is still acid and will cause significant damage to you and/or your clothing! Handle with extreme caution! You should <u>always</u> wear safety goggles when working with batteries. (**Comment:** Cotton clothing is eaten up/destroyed by battery acid, but Polyester is not affected. [Where are the old 1970's clothes when you need them?])

When you look at an RV battery, the first thing you notice is the high-impact plastic casing (the color is purely aesthetic). Next, you notice the filler caps – these caps protect/cover the holes in the top of the casing. They may be individual caps or a set of caps affixed together.

Finally, you will notice the thick lead terminals (posts) sticking out from the top cover – one on each end of the battery. One post will be marked with a positive ("+") sign and the other with a negative ("−") sign.

Each one of the holes in the top covering is an access opening to one of the battery's "cells." A 12-Volt Battery has six openings – therefore, six cells, whereas a 6-Volt Battery only has three holes – dot, dot, daa. (**Comment:** A battery is called a "battery" because it is a battery [combination] of cells bound together to produce a single electrical effect.) A cell is made up of a series of "plates" and "separators."

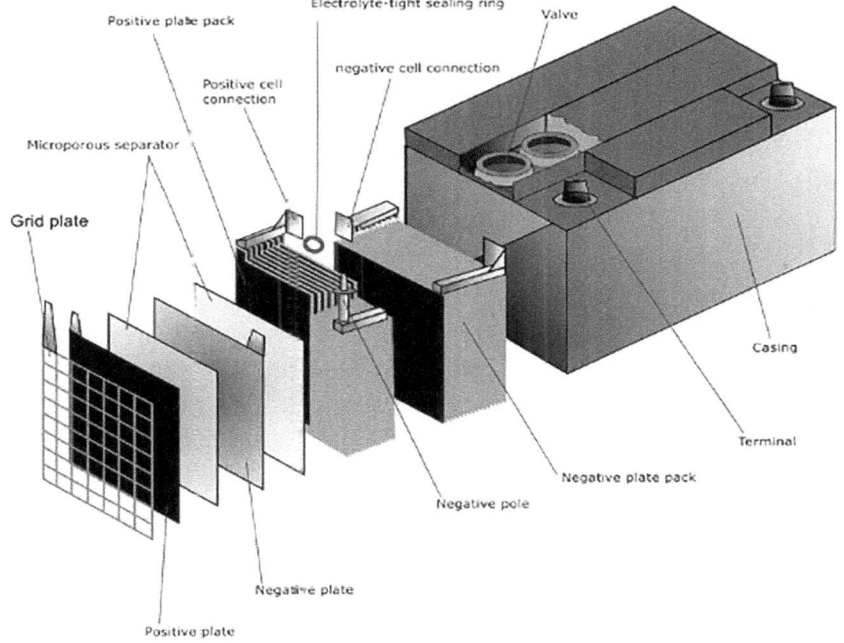

[source: ustudy.in]

The **plates** are metal grids (they resemble thin, square waffles) and are covered with a lead paste – a mixture of lead and other materials. The paste on the positive plates is Lead Dioxide (PbO_2) (also referred to as lead peroxide) and has a light orangish-brown color. The Lead paste (Pb) on the negative plates looks "spongy" in nature and slate gray. The number and thickness of plates in each cell depends on the "application" of the battery (see Page 31).

The positive plates are uniquely connected to a positive plate pack, as are the negative plates into a negative plate pack. The positive and negative plate packs are then interlaced together ("+" plate | "−" plate | "+" plate | "−" plate | etc.), and this arrangement constitutes the **"cell."**

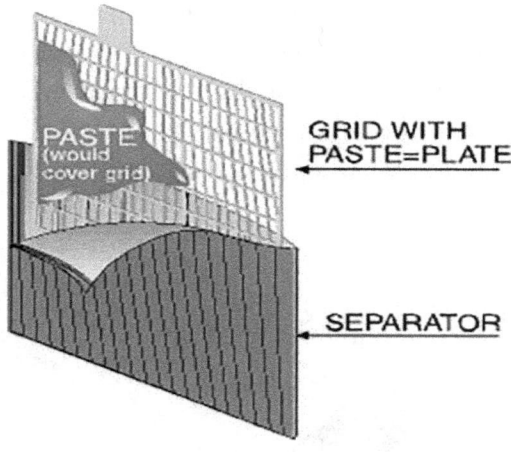

[source: batterycouncil.org]

In between the plates is a **separator** made of a microporous, non-conducting material. This separator prevents the positive and negative plates from touching each other and short-circuiting. Its porosity allows for the easy flow of the electrolyte between all of the plates.

Each cell is enclosed within a separate compartment inside the case. (Yes, that's why every cell has its own access opening and why the electrolyte cannot flow from cell to cell.) Each cell is electronically connected in "series" to the next cell. That means that the positive battery terminal/post on the top is connected to the positive plate pack of the cell directly below it. Then, that same cell's negative plate pack connector is attached to the positive plate pack of the next cell. This "series" connection continues all the way to the negative battery terminal/post at the other end.

That gives us a "**Charging**" electrical path that looks like this:

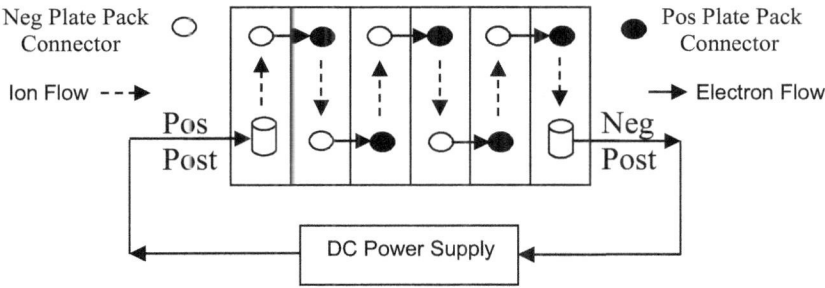

Series connection of cells — a top-down view

This electrical path is unique because the electrical current flows as ions (charged molecules in the acid) between the plates and flows as electrons through the physical connections between the cells. (Now, that's some pretty neat stuff!!!!) But how does the "magic" really occur?

When a Lead-Acid Battery is initially built and filled with electrolyte, it does **not** have a charge or polarity. How does that happen? Well, right after the battery has finished being assembled, everything is neutral – chemically and electrically – there is no interaction between the elements. Think of "neutral" as "dead" (or another term – "flat"). That's because there is no electrical potential between the plates themselves, and the electrolyte is non-reactive to the plate materials. Therefore, the cells are stable. In reality, the battery is manufactured in a discharged state. An external electrical charge must be applied to the battery in order to start the first chemical reaction.

Whoa, there! Those last two sentences force us to debunk another common misconception. Contrary to popular belief, a battery *does not make or produce electricity* all by itself. A battery is merely a two-way (in & out) storage container – something is put in and later taken out (think in terms of your RV's freshwater tank – it doesn't make the water; the holding tanks – they don't make the waste, or the fuel tank – it doesn't make the diesel or gasoline). As unique chemical reactions in the battery occur, electrical energy is either stored or released. And conveniently for us, with today's rechargeable batteries, this process can be repeated over and over again.

So..., a robust electrical charge is applied to a newly built battery. Inside the battery, this electrical charge will cause some chemical reactions to take place. However, in order to initiate these chemical reactions, the manufacturer, when building the battery, actually has to add a coat of a soft, paste-like substance called Lead Sulfate ($PbSO_4$) to all of the plates. And, the electrolyte installed is initially weaker (more water, less acid) than normal.

When the battery begins charging, the positive plates accept electrons from the external source. This, in turn, causes a chain reaction of all the chemical components in the cells. They get really excited and begin to react with one another. (Think in terms of the effect that hard-rock music has at a fraternity/sorority party.) In fact, the lead sulfate and water molecules begin to break down, shift around, and start transforming back into both metallic (sponge) lead on the negative plates and sulfuric acid or lead dioxide on the positive plates and sulfuric acid. These conditions are considered natural states. Ultimately, the chemical reaction reaches a point where nothing else can occur. When this saturation point is reached, ta-daa, we have a fully charged battery!

Here is the "charging" chemical equation for the chemistry enthusiasts is the crowd: $2\ PbSO_4 + 2\ H_2O \longrightarrow 2\ H_2SO_4 + PbO_2 + Pb$.

Special Note: One particular chemical reaction that occurs during charging (or recharging) is called **gassing**. Gassing is the production of hydrogen gas caused by the charge current breaking down the water in the electrolyte. This released hydrogen gas is vented to the atmosphere through the filler caps. Steady gassing is _**normal**_ during the charging process. The loss of hydrogen results in the loss of water. Why? Because it takes two hydrogen molecules and one oxygen molecule to make water (H_2O). And, since there will be less hydrogen available to reconstitute water, the need to "add water" to your battery/ies regularly becomes intuitively obvious. (See, I told you at the beginning of this _**Primer**_ that I would answer the question of "what does that have to do with anything.") And there will be more information on this subject forthcoming.

Special WARNING: Contrary to popular belief, <u>NEVER</u> remove the caps when charging a battery. Except when watering the battery, the caps should always be left in place. PERIOD. (The vents in the caps meter the release of hydrogen. This diagram provides a good "technical" view of the vent caps and the recommended spacing between the plate tops and the vent.)

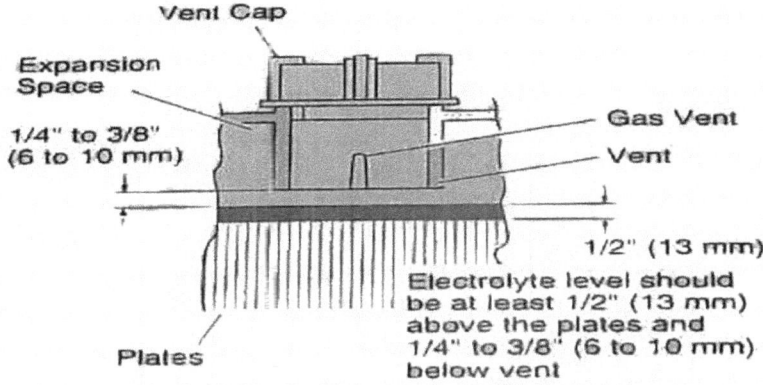

[source: mountaintopgolfcars.com]

Extra Special WARNING: Many Lead-Acid Battery explosions are believed to occur when the electrolyte level is below the top of the plates in the cell(s), thus creating a "large" space that allows hydrogen gas to accumulate in heavy concentration. When a low electrolyte battery is engaged with a load, it may spark internally between the exposed positive and negative plates. This spark ignites the amassed hydrogen gas and causes the battery to explode. "BOOM!!"

Really Extra Special WARNING: Keep open flames, sparks, and/or electric arcs out of your battery compartment. That even means cell phones! And remember, hydrogen gas is extremely flammable – definitely NO SMOKING anywhere near any RV battery bank!!!!!!! (Yes, that applies especially to <u>you</u>.)

Now, back to how our RV battery works...

Although a charged battery can "sit" for quite a while without a demand or recharge, the battery will, very gradually, start self-discharging. This means that the chemical state is slowly returning to its original neutral state.

But what happens inside the battery when a load is drawn from it? Let's say some lights, the water pump, and a vent fan motor are turned on. (Hello, Houston, we have a demand for 12-Volt power.)

A "**Discharge**" electrical path looks like this:

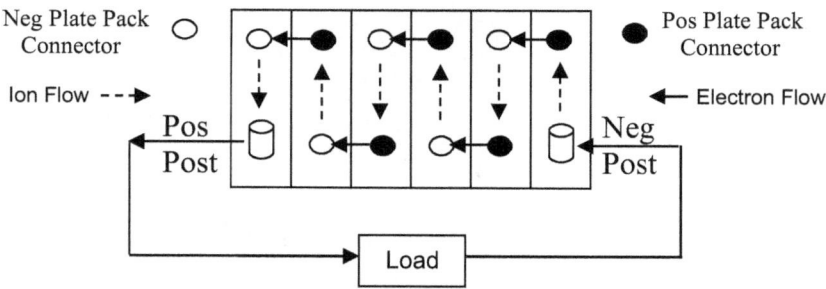

Series connection of cells — a top-down view

First, let me say that the "discharge" electrical path is just the opposite of the "charge" path – it flows from negative to positive <u>inside the battery</u>! So, that means our electrical draw "starts" at the negative terminal/post, flows toward the positive terminal/post, and then externally to the load. (Yep, it's a Law of Physics, so just accept it.)

Logically, it <u>must</u> start at the negative terminal/post because each cell can only produce approximately 2.11 Volts. And, since the cells are connected in series, the voltage is cumulative. Therefore, six (6) cells in series, at 2.11 volts each, accumulate to a total of around 12.66 Volts, leaving the positive post to power the load. (Hmm... must be one of those "12-Volt" batteries.)

Chemically, in response to the load's demand for current, the following reactions occur inside the battery:

1. Lead (Pb) molecules on the negative plates combine with Sulfate (SO_4) molecules to create Lead Sulfate ($PbSO_4$) and some free electrons.

2. Lead Dioxide (PbO_2), Hydrogen ions, Sulfate ions, plus some of the free electrons from the lead (negative) plates combine to create Lead Sulfate and water on the Lead Dioxide (positive) plates.

3. As the battery continues to discharge, both plates build up a layer of Lead Sulfate. Water also builds up in the electrolyte.

The process of the sponge lead (negative plate) being eaten away by the sulfuric acid and changing to hydrogen and lead sulfate is the basis of the battery discharging. The positive plate does not enter into the chemical reaction taking place at all. It merely provides an exit path for the current.

When a battery is fully discharged, the negative plates retain some sponge lead. The positive plates retain some lead dioxide. But the amount of lead sulfate on each plate is maximized. The sulfuric acid in the electrolyte has been reduced to a minimal amount. When this condition is reached, no further chemical action can take place. A neutral state has been achieved.

Here is the "discharging" chemical equation for the chemists still in the crowd: $2 H_2SO_4 + PbO_2 + Pb \longrightarrow 2 PbSO_4 + 2 H_2O$

Did you notice that the chemical equations for charging and discharging are exact opposites? That's why we can charge and discharge a Lead-Acid Battery repeatedly until the elements physically wear out.

Here is one more physics truth: Batteries are not 100% efficient. Some energy is lost as heat from chemical reactions during the charging and discharging processes.

Okay, that about covers the subject of battery basics. Now, on to more specific information...especially information that debunks the concept of any battery being a "maintenance free" battery. Trust me when I say, "They do NOT exist!"

Do I really need to add water to the house battery/ies??

YES – as stated earlier in this *Primer*, you <u>must</u> keep an eye on the electrolyte (liquid) level in the battery/ies and add water as necessary!

(**Comment:** According to *BatteryStuff.com*, "Approximately 50% of all <u>premature</u> battery failures are caused by the loss of water from regular recharging, the lack of maintenance, evaporation from high heat, or especially when overcharging.")

As a matter of habit, you should regularly check each cell of your House Battery Bank level. I check mine religiously on the first of each month. However, in a hot climate (> 85°F), the most dangerous and unforgiving environment for any battery, you will need to check all of the cell's electrolyte levels more often – at least twice a month or even more often if the outside ambient temperature is around 100°F.

Caution: Do <u>not</u> add any acid to any battery to bring the electrolyte back up to an appropriate level — that's just a waste of your money and can certainly kill the battery prematurely. All you add is water – **ONLY distilled or de-ionized water** — and make sure you do not overfill any of the cells!

BUT WAIT…before you add any water, charge the battery/ies FIRST!! That's right; if you maintain your electrolyte level regularly, you should charge <u>first</u> and then top off to the correct level. Adding water before charging can cause a significant overflowing of the electrolyte while charging. **Critical Note:** Only add water <u>before</u> charging <u>if</u> the tops of the plates are exposed. Avoid overfilling, especially in hot climates, because heat will cause the electrolyte to expand and overflow.

Again, a few words of Caution about treating batteries with the consideration, as well as the apprehension, they demand:

Remember: The battery's electrolyte contains Sulfuric Acid, a highly corrosive, strong mineral acid capable of causing very severe burns. Consequently, protective clothing, gloves, and safety glasses are always recommended to shield you in case of an accidental spill out or splash-back. (BTW – never open the battery caps with your face directly over the battery.) If such an accident does occur, immediately rinse the affected area(s) with large quantities of cold water for at least ten to fifteen minutes to mitigate the acid's corrosive effect on your eye(s) and/or skin.

Also, Remember: All charging batteries produce flammable hydrogen gas and can explode violently (like a bomb) if the gas is ignited. This is especially important when batteries are housed inside any compartment (which they usually are). So make sure the compartment is well ventilated. And **NEVER** use spark generating (steel) tools, allow open flames, or smoke tobacco products anywhere near your battery/bank. And, absolutely, never lay a metal tool down on the top of any battery.

Let's now talk about "Sulfation" — one of those terms that everyone hears, but no one seems to know what it means. Too many "battery experts" (a.k.a. "proverbial campfire techs") attribute every premature battery failure to sulfation. The actual number is down around 80%, and this applies primarily to batteries that are not used at least once a week. Long storage time without proper charging is detrimental to all batteries. (Please *remember* that.)

Sulfation is an integral part of a battery's chemical reaction process. It is the transformation of Lead and Sulfuric Acid into Lead Sulfate (Earlier, we explored how this occurs during the discharge cycle.) Lead Sulfate is a soft crystal that generally forms in the nooks and crannies of the surfaces of both types of plates.

However, sulfation becomes a problem when a battery is:

1. Left for any length of time in a discharged condition,

2. Continually undercharged, or

3. The electrolyte level has dropped below the top of the plates.

If any of these conditions occur, some soft lead sulfate begins to crystallize into hard lead sulfate. As it advances towards a crystalline state, it expands. Because the lead sulfate enters the pores on the plates, the crystal growth causes plate material to break off, much the same way as the formation of ice in a crack of a rock will cause pieces of the rock to break off. Once this happens, these hard crystals cannot be reconverted during any subsequent recharging cycles, nor can the broken-off plate material be reaffixed.

The longer sulfation occurs, the larger and more complex the lead sulfate crystals will become. (Remember the old crystal growing science fair project – possibly yours?)

Magnified Sulfation Crystals of PbSO4
[source: Wikipedia.com]

These permanent crystals significantly affect the charging cycle, resulting in longer charging times, less efficient and incomplete charging, and higher battery temperatures. (Higher temperature speeds up sulfation, and too much heat damages the battery by accelerating corrosion.) Ultimately, the battery will die a premature death.

Sulfation Prevention can be accomplished in one of three ways:

1. Always keep the battery connected to an external charger. This charger should be capable of delivering a continuous temperature compensated "float" charge at the battery. This type of charger is not just a cheap "trickle" charger because of

2. the temperature compensation feature. (If you have four or more "house" batteries, check out the 2 Bank or 4 Bank Battery Tender Charging Stations at *www.batterytender.com*)

   Note: Physically disconnect your House Battery (bank) when using an external charger. That means removing the negative (usually black) cable from the battery ("–") terminal. You know, the cable that is connected to Ground (the chassis).

3. Periodically recharge the battery when the charge level drops to 80% or less. On an "open-circuit" battery, this means at or below 12.51 volts. (A good digital voltmeter will give you the necessary two digits after the decimal point.) Just make sure it is an open-circuit test.

4. Possibly use a solar panel specifically designed to "float" charge a battery. **Caution:** If you connect a solar panel directly to a battery, it will eventually overcharge the battery and damage it. That's why you need to use a solar charge controller. (**Comment**: Most sole purpose [trickle or float charging] solar panels currently on the market are only designed to charge one [1] battery at a time. There isn't a "one panel does it all" solar system out there [yet] that can adequately charge an RV's Deep-Cycle "house" battery bank – you need at least one [1] 45-watt panel for each Deep-Cycle Battery in the bank.)

If you are interested in serious **Solar Battery Charging** for your RV and/or living "off the grid," I highly recommend *www.amsolar.com* for an in-depth education on solar power. They do a much better presentation than I could hope to do. (BTW – solar power is trendy west of the Mississippi River and not so popular east of the Mississippi [too many trees in the East].)

SERVICING BATTERIES

According to the University of Wisconsin System (*wisconsin.edu*), here a just a few things to pay attention to when servicing batteries:

- Keep metal tools and jewelry away from the battery.

- Inspect for defective cables, loose connections, corroded cable connectors or battery terminals, cracked cases or covers, loose hold-down clamps, and deformed or loosed terminal posts.

- Replace worn or unserviceable parts.

- Check the charge level of non-sealed and sealed batteries with an accurate digital voltmeter. Do this when not plugged into shore power, the engine is not running, and lights or other electrically powered equipment are turned off. Also, check the electrolyte levels and specific gravity in each cell of non-sealed batteries.

- When checking the electrolyte liquid levels of the battery/ies, use a rated flashlight that won't cause a spark. In the event one is not available, use a plastic/non-metallic flashlight. Turn "ON" the flashlight before getting near the battery when checking cell levels, and turn "OFF" the flashlight when you are away from the batteries.

- Tighten cable clamp nuts with the proper size wrench. Avoid subjecting battery terminals to excessive twisting forces.

- Use a cable puller to remove a cable clamp from the battery terminal.

- Remove corrosion on the terminal posts, hold-down tray, and hold-down parts.

- Use a tapered brush to clean battery terminals and the cable clamps.

- Wash and clean the battery, battery terminals, and case or tray with water. The corrosive acid can be neutralized by brushing

- on some baking soda (sodium bicarbonate) solution. If the solution does not bubble, the acid is probably neutralized. Rinse the battery with water to remove the baking soda solution.

- To prevent shocks, never touch or come in contact with both terminals at the same time. For example, if a baking soda solution is applied with a cloth, remember that these solutions can conduct electricity.

- When battery cables are removed, ensure that they are clearly marked "positive" and "negative" so that they are reconnected with the correct polarity.

- Use a battery carrier to lift a battery or place hands at opposite corners. Remember, Deep-Cycle Batteries can weigh 60 to 65 pounds each, so practice safe lifting and carrying procedures to prevent back injuries.

- Use a self-leveling filler that automatically fills the battery to a predetermined level. Never fill battery cells above the level indicator.

- If you use a syringe device (like a turkey baster) to add water to a battery, do not squeeze the bulb so hard that the water you are adding splashes acid out of the cell opening.

BATTERY TERMINAL CORROSION

Corrosion appears as a white, ashy deposit typically around the positive or, possibly, both battery posts. Sometimes there is also a bit of color mixed in. These deposits result from several possible chemical exchanges involving electrons, vapors, and the lead battery post. This corrosion will absolutely stop the flow of electricity from the battery to any load. The build-up of corrosion means you need to check and clean the battery terminals more often.

Here is a very good battery terminal cleaning technique from *howtocleanstuff.net*:

How to Clean Battery Terminals

Supplies:

- A combination tool – battery post brush and battery clamp brush, and/or a small-handled wire brush. Both are obtainable at any auto parts store or online.

Combination Tool

Small Handled Wire Brush

- Locking pliers (vice grips)
- Toothbrush
- Baking soda
- Water
- Clean, lint-free cloth
- Open-end Wrenches
- Grease or petroleum jelly

Directions:

Remove the battery cables from the battery terminals by loosening the nut on each cable clamp. (Use the right-sized open-end wrench – **not** a crescent wrench.) Once they are loose, *always remove the cable clamp from the negative terminal first.* It's marked with a minus ("–") sign; the positive terminal has a plus ("+") sign. The cable clamp may not come off easily. You will have to wiggle it and lift it upward until the clamp comes off the terminal post.

Sometimes, especially if there is a lot of corrosion, you may need the assistance of a pair of locking pliers. Be careful not to touch any tool you use against anything metal (like the compartment wall) when that tool is in contact with the battery's positive post. (Think in terms of Arcing and Sparking!)

1. Examine the battery cables and clamps for excess wear or corrosion. Should damage appear extensive, replace the cables and clamps to avoid future problems.

2. Check the battery case for cracks and the terminals for damage. If you find either, replace the battery.

3. Secure the loose cables so that they don't accidentally flop back onto the terminals.

4. Pour some baking soda solution directly onto the posts.

5. Dip a toothbrush in water and use it to scrub the baking soda into the terminal posts and cable clamps. Skin and eye protection are strongly recommended.

6. If the toothbrush isn't doing the job, use one of your battery terminal cleaner brushes on it. Also, shine up the insides of the cable clamps by using the clamp cleaner that usually comes attached to the terminal brush or use a plain, soap-free steel wool pad.

7. Dry everything off with a clean, disposable, lint-free rag.

8. Smear grease or petroleum jelly on the posts to slow down the formation of corrosive deposits. Also, cover all exposed metal surfaces on the battery posts, battery cables, and clamps.

9. Replace the positive clamp first and then replace the negative clamp (just the opposite of how you took them off). Next, tighten them down with the proper sized wrench. Crescent wrenches are NOT recommended – they tend to round off the points on the nuts if they are not tight and slip off.

The following is a combination of several articles from *ehow.com*:

How to Clean and Add Water to a Deep-Cycle Battery

Things you'll need:

- Baking soda
- Warm water
- Measuring cup
- Pair of latex gloves
- Safety glasses
- Soft brush
- Paper towels or clean lint-free rags
- Standard screwdriver
- Flashlight, if necessary
- Distilled water

Instructions:

1. Prepare a solution using the following ratio: one tablespoon of baking soda to eight ounces of warm water.

2. Open the door to the battery compartment. Put on a pair of latex gloves and safety glasses. They will help keep battery acid off your hands and out of your eyes during the cleaning procedure.

3. Apply the baking soda solution to the top of the battery with a soft brush to remove dust, grease, and acid residue. Next, wipe the top of the battery clean with a paper towel or clean rag. Cleaning the battery will neutralize any acid residue and prevent water contamination inside the battery during your inspection.

4. Unscrew or pry off the filler caps from the top of the battery with the standard screwdriver. Then, carefully wipe off any dirt from the battery filler holes with a clean paper towel or rag.

5. Look into each battery filler hole and make sure the water level covers the top of the battery plates and separators.

(Remember, each cell has its own filler hole.) If necessary, use a flashlight to help you see the actual water level. If your battery has fill rings, which are basically an extension of the filler hole walls and are used as a level indicator, make sure the water level reaches the bottom of the fill rings.

6. As necessary, add distilled water to every cell to cover the top of the battery plates and separators or bring the level up to the bottom of the fill rings.

7. Replace the filler caps on the battery, throw away the latex gloves, and close the compartment.

HAVING A PROBLEM WATERING YOUR BATTERY/IES?

The most common excuses that I hear from RVers about why they don't add water to their battery/ies are – "The battery/ies in the 'back' are too hard to get to," or "It's too tight in there, and I can't see into the filler holes," or "I have to take them out each time, and they're too heavy," or the worst one, yet, "It just takes too much time."

Well, my friends, there is an answer to everyone's prayer. What you need to get is an **onboard battery watering system**. Once such a system is installed, it will take less than two minutes to water as many as six House Batteries.

(**Comment:** I installed such a system in my own rig as soon as they became available for RVs. [They were on the golf course for a long time before they came to RVs.] I can water my House Battery Bank of four [4] batteries in less than a minute and a half. All I have to do is drop the pump's suction line into a bottle of distilled water and start squeezing to prime the tube with water. Once the tube is full, I hook up my squeeze pump to the end of the system's attached filler tube and start pumping again. When the pump is "firm" [can't squeeze it anymore], I stop. The process is complete. How simple is that?)

Here's what an installed battery watering system may look like:

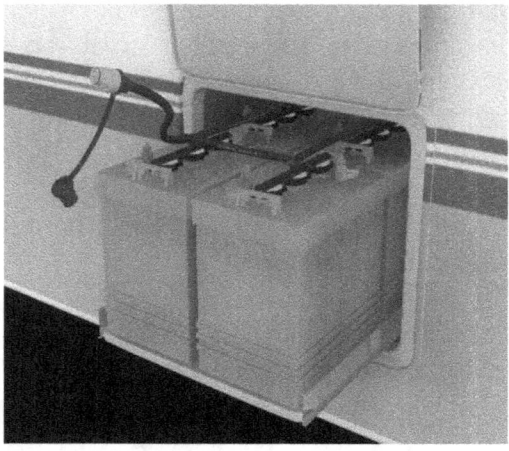

[source: flow-rite.com]

Just how does this battery watering system work? The filler caps are replaced with "snorkel" devices (the manufacturer calls them *valves*) that fit into the filler holes. Each snorkel extends into the cell to a precise depth. (**Note:** The newer snorkels include a water barrier and flame arrester. The arrester prevents a flame from entering adjacent cells should accidental cell gas ignition occur [see Page 16].) All of the snorkels on one battery are attached to a common manifold. Each manifold has a 3-port swivel "T" mounted on the top. The manifolds from separate batteries are connected via rubber tubing (running from one "T" to another) in a "series" fashion. The unused ports on the "T's" are capped off. A specialized connection tube that mates with the pump is also attached to one of the "T's."

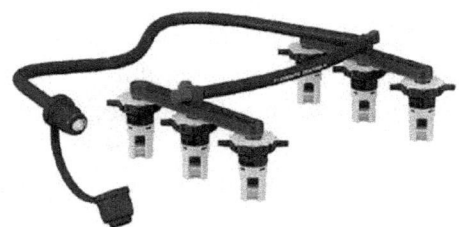

[source: flow-rite.com]

When the pump is attached and squeezed, water is added to each cell. The snorkel automatically shuts off the water flow into a cell when full (just like a ball-type swimming snorkel shuts off the water flow when you go under the surface). When all the cells are full, you cannot pump any more water.

[source: flow-rite.com]

(**Comment:** When I install one of these systems for a customer, it usually takes me about an hour and a half to complete a four [4] battery bank system. Since I'm already elbow deep into the battery compartment, I get very particular and always clean the battery top, terminals, and cable connections before installing the watering system and top off the cells. [I'm a firm believer in "full" battery service and maintenance.])

Well, now, let's get back to some more generic information about batteries...

There are two different uses for batteries in RVs.

> **Motorhome Chassis Battery.** The battery (or batteries in diesel units) used to start the engine is called the Chassis Battery (or Main Battery). It only has one purpose – to start the engine. This battery is usually called a "maintenance-free" type. (Although there isn't such a thing as a maintenance-free battery – as you recognized while reading the previous "servicing" and "cleaning" sections of this *Primer*.) Here, "maintenance free" only means that you can't add water.

> **House Battery.** The battery (or battery bank) used to provide electrical power to the 12-Volt lights and some appliances is called the House Battery (or Auxiliary Battery). Unfortunately, this battery (or bank) tends to be the most neglected component in any RV!!! **Note:** This battery (or bank) is also used to start the onboard generator in a motorhome.

TYPES OF BATTERIES

Batteries are categorized by application (what they are used for) and construction (how they are built).

The major **applications** are: **Automotive** and **Deep-Cycle**

Automotive Batteries (also referred to as "SLI" Batteries – <u>S</u>tarter, <u>L</u>ighting, and <u>I</u>gnition) are designed for one primary purpose – to start engines. The associated Starter Motor requires a short burst of high current to operate successfully. In order to do this, Automotive Batteries are made with a substantial number of thin plates in order to maximize the surface area of lead exposed to the electrolyte and therefore provide maximum current output.

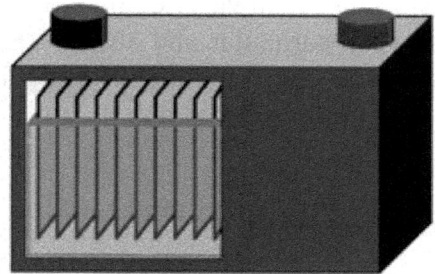

[source: cadex.com]

Automotive Batteries are typically "maintenance-free" batteries (no openings to add water). However, they can only withstand about 15 to 30 deep cycles because of their thin plates. For this reason, Automotive Batteries are **NOT** recommended for use as RV House Batteries. (**Comment:** Although cheaper, they don't give you the best bang for your buck.)

Deep-Cycle Batteries are designed to power electrical equipment for long periods of time. They can actually be discharged <u>almost</u> to a maximum of 80%, repeatedly. The significant difference between a Deep-Cycle Battery and others is that they have thicker plates that typically deliver less peak current but can withstand frequent discharging.

[source: cadex.com]

This type of battery is usually found in RVs that have inverters. Although a Deep-Cycle Battery is considered, by many, to be very expensive, they still offer the best price to power/lifespan ratio (a.k.a. "best bang for the buck").

Another type of application, the **RV/Marine Battery,** is actually a "Dual Purpose Battery" and falls somewhere between the Starting and Deep-Cycle Batteries. In a Dual Purpose Battery, the plates are made similar to those used in Automotive Batteries but somewhat thicker. "Dual Purpose Batteries" should not be discharged more than 50% anytime during their lifespan.

This type of battery is usually rated as a 12-Volt Battery and is found in entry-level RVs – be they motorhomes, travel trailers, or fifth-wheels.

(**Comment:** The "Dual Purpose Battery" was originally designed for the Boating Industry and initially referred to as a Marine Battery. Large boats with cabins require a battery to start the engine[s] and provide power to a few lights or appliances. The RV industry adopted the Dual Purpose Batteries because they are cheaper than Deep-Cycle Batteries and provide a "reasonable" amount of 12-Volt power for a "limited" amount of time, hence the new "RV/Marine" name.)

Suppose you have a Dual Purpose 12-Volt System. In that case, I recommend upgrading to a Deep-Cycle 12-Volt System (two Deep-Cycle 6-Volt Batteries connected in series) if you plan on going to do any significant amount of RVing.

The key battery **construction** types are: **Flooded**, **Gel**, **AGM**, and **LFP**.

Since we have already discussed flooded batteries in great detail, let's talk about the other three types of construction.

Gel Cell Batteries have the same basic structural design as flooded batteries. The major difference is the electrolyte. The electrolyte in this battery's cells is suspended in a silica-type gel (sort of like stiff Jell-O, initially, and then like peanut brittle after a break-in phase). This thick paste-like material allows electrons to flow between the plates. Fortunately, if the casing is broken, the gel will not leak out.

AGM Batteries are our latest generation of Lead-Acid Batteries. They also have the same basic structural design as flooded batteries. However, the electrolyte in this type of battery is <u>A</u>bsorbed in a <u>G</u>lass <u>M</u>atte – a specialized fiberglass separator designed to wick the electrolyte between the plates and thereby allow electrons to flow. Thus, if the battery casing is broken, there is no free liquid inside to leak out. (**Comment:** The Deep-Cycle AGMs are far better for RVing than the Automotive AGMs — for the same reason, "maintenance-free" Automotive Batteries are not recommended for use as RV House Batteries!)

While both the Gel Cell and AGM batteries are somewhat pricey, they also have some distinctive advantages:

1. The oxygen evolved at the positive plates will recombine with the Hydrogen developed at the negative plates to create water. (That's a fancy way of explaining why you don't need to add water to either type.)

2. Neither type of battery needs to be kept upright. Instead, they can be mounted sideways, if necessary.

3. Neither type of battery needs to be vented to the atmosphere. (Since the Hydrogen cannot escape, there is no explosive gas escaping.)

4. They are incredibly high vibration resistant.

5. The self-discharge rate is significantly less than flooded batteries.

There is, however, one major drawback:

Both types of batteries are susceptible to overcharging. Therefore, these batteries must be charged correctly, or they will suffer irreparable damage and premature failure! **Note:** If you are using either of these types of batteries with an inverter, make sure you adjust the charge rate to the type of battery you have!! If you don't, you <u>will</u> be buying new batteries sooner than you think.

And, now, the newest rage in the RV community — **Lithium Ferro Phosphate Batteries** (LFP)

Like the Lead-Acid Battery/ies, in the LFP battery/ies, lithium ions migrate from the negative plate through an electrolyte to the positive plate during discharge and back when charging. However, unlike the Lead-Acid Battery/ies, LFPs use a lithium iron phosphate ($LiFePO_4$) compound on the positive plates and typically graphitic carbon on the negative plates. Also, the LFP battery/ies typically only have four (4) cells, thus, taking up less space.

PROS:

LFP batteries have a very constant discharge voltage (3.2V per Cell), no memory effect, and low self-discharge — all with no fumes and no venting.

Because they are smaller, LFPs weigh about 1/3 to 1/2 the weight of Lead-Acid Batteries of equal capacity.

LFPs have an approximate 99% charge efficiency vs. Lead-Acid's approximate 85%, seemingly charging 4 to 6 times faster.

LFPs reportedly last 2 to 4 times longer than Lead-Acid Batteries.

CON:

Super Expensive! They cost 3 to 4 times more than AGM batteries.

(**Comment:** If you think that serious "off-the-grid" RVing is something you want to do, I earnestly recommend you research all the types of Deep Cycle Batteries, to the Nth degree, before you take any financial plunge.)

A battery's **rating** is annotated in several different ways, depending on the battery type. (The following rating definitions are from *dcbattery.com*)

"Starting Batteries are rated in terms of Cold Cranking Amps (CCA). The CCA rating characterizes 'the maximum amperes that can be continuously removed from a battery for 30 seconds at 0°F before its voltage drops to unusable levels." Understandably, the higher the CCA rating, the greater the starting power of the battery.

"Deep-Cycle Batteries are rated in terms of Ampere-Hours (AH). The AH rating 'for battery capacity is obtained by multiplying the current flow in amperes by the time in hours of discharge. Example: A battery that delivers 5 Amps for 20 hours would have a 100 Amp-Hour battery rating ($5 \times 20 = 100$)'." A 6-Volt Deep-Cycle RV Battery is typically rated at 225 Amp-Hours.

Now for those of you concerned with getting the biggest bang for your buck, here are some typical life expectancies for batteries used in Deep-Cycle (RV House Battery) service:

- Automotive   0 -12 months *
- RV/Marine   2 - 4 years *
- Golf cart   3 - 5 years *
- RV Deep-Cycle   7 - 10 years *
- Gelled Deep-Cycle 4 - 8 years **
- AGM Deep-Cycle   2 -10 years **
- LFP Deep-Cycle   5 – 7 years

* Remember – these life expectancies are based on proper maintenance, watering, and battery charging.

** Proper maintenance and charging still apply.

Battery Freshness is something you will probably need to consider when purchasing new/replacement battery/ies for your RV. The following is an interesting statement from *nationallibertyalliance.org*:

"Determining the freshness of a battery is sometimes difficult. Never buy a wet Lead-Acid Battery that is more than three months old! Because, by then, it has started to sulfate unless it has been periodically recharged (this is not the usual practice of many retailers)."

"The exceptions to this recommendation are AGM and Gel Cell batteries, which can be stored up to 12 months before the charge level drops to 80% or below."

"Dealers will often place their older batteries at the front of the display racks so they will sell first. The newest batteries can often be found at the rear of the rack or in a storage room. The date of manufacture is usually stamped into the case or printed on an affixed sticker."

Most battery manufacturers stamp a date code on the top of the battery. It's almost always the first number and first letter.

B = February
7 = 2007

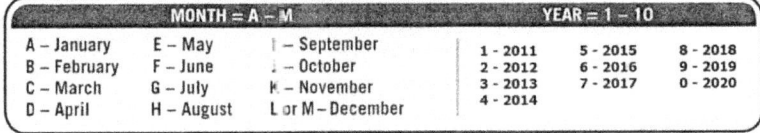

MONTH = A – M			YEAR = 1 – 10		
A – January	E – May	I – September	1 - 2011	5 - 2015	8 - 2018
B – February	F – June	J – October	2 - 2012	6 - 2016	9 - 2019
C – March	G – July	K – November	3 - 2013	7 - 2017	0 - 2020
D – April	H – August	L or M – December	4 - 2014		

Or, you may find a date sticker on the top or side that looks like this:

[source: interstatebatteries.com & modified by Author]

RV HOUSE BATTERY CHARGING

RV House Battery charging is a great deal less complicated than it used to be. The engineering has progressed significantly to improve how RV batteries are being charged. The newest chargers on the market are 3-stage chargers referred to as "Smart Chargers."

When a **3-stage charger** is "online," battery charging is accomplished in three separate but progressive stages: Bulk, Acceptance/Absorption, and Float.

Let's take a look at each stage:

Bulk Charge: The 1st stage of 3-stage battery charging.

Current is sent to the battery/ies at the maximum safe rate they will accept until the battery voltage rises to nearly 80% of its full charge level. Voltages at this stage typically range from 12.7 volts to 15 volts – depending on the battery's ambient temperature. As a rule of thumb, the charge voltage <u>must</u> be higher than the actual charge level of the battery. You obviously cannot charge a battery with a charge level of 12.4 volts with only 11.5 charging volts. (***Remember:*** Bulk Charge = Increasing Voltage and Constant High Current.)

(**Comment:** Every time an RV is connected to shore power or generator power, the converter/charger will automatically start in this mode. If the battery bank has been deeply discharged, this will result in a high amp draw on the 120 VAC side of the converter/charger. This high demand <u>plus</u> any additional demand for 120 VAC current may cause a post/pedestal breaker to "trip" unexpectedly. Turn off the other loads until the converter/charger shifts into the Acceptance/Absorption mode – especially if plugged into a 30 Amp outlet.)

Acceptance/Absorption Charge: The 2nd stage of 3-stage battery charging.

Voltage remains constant, and current gradually tapers off as internal resistance increases during charging. It is during this stage that the charger puts out maximum voltage. Voltages at this stage are typically around 14.2 to 15.5 volts. (**Remember:** Acceptance/Absorption Charge = Constant High Voltage and Decreasing Current.)

Float Charge: The 3rd stage of 3-stage battery charging.

After the battery/ies reach their full charge, charging voltage is reduced to a lower level (typically 12.8 to 13.2 volts) to minimize gassing and prolong battery life. This is often referred to as a maintenance or trickle charge because it aims to keep an already charged battery from discharging. (**Remember:** Float Charge = Constant Voltage and Maintenance Current.) The converter/charger will usually remain in the Float mode until it is disconnected from incoming AC power.

This is what 3-Stage Charging looks like graphically:

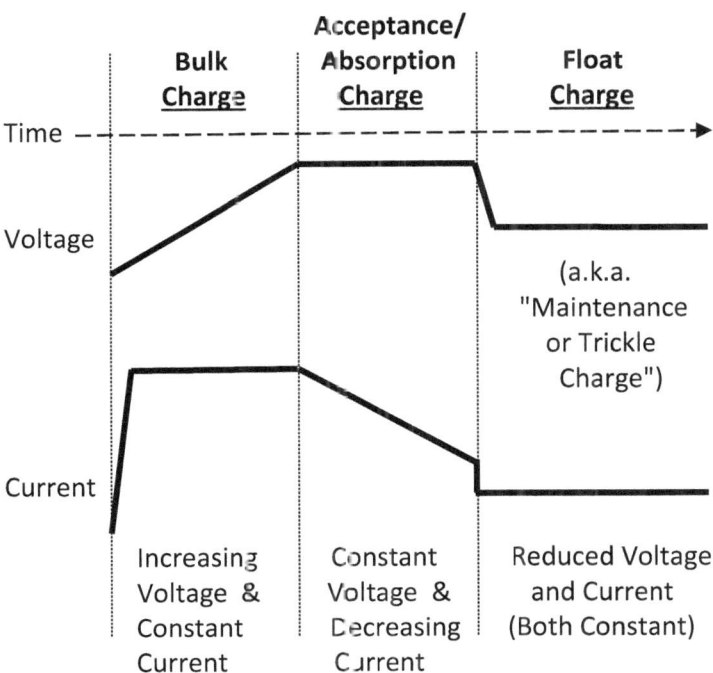

The Ten Commandments for Batteries

- Thou shall not neglect thy battery/ies. Perform all maintenance and service responsibilities regularly.

- Thou shall use a 3-Stage charger for the best results.

- Thou shall choose the appropriate charge levels for Lead-Acid, Gel Cell, and AGM batteries. Check the manufacturer's specifications for recommended voltage thresholds.

- Thou shall prevent Sulfation. Charge Lead-Acid Battery/ies after each use – do not store a battery that is low on charge or low on electrolyte.

- Thou shall not charge any battery with the caps removed.

- Thou shall not smoke nor generate sparks near any battery/ies! Hydrogen gas produced during charging is explosive.

- Thou shall not kill. Most of the RV "House" batteries do not die from old age; they are annihilated, in their prime, by neglect!

- Thou shall water thy battery/ies regularly. Only add **Distilled** or **De-Ionized Water** to a battery.

- Thou shall not add acid to any battery.

- Thou shall not allow a Lead-Acid Battery to freeze. A discharged battery freezes sooner than one that is fully charged. **Warning:** Never attempt to charge a frozen battery.

BATTERY INSPECTION

Visual inspection of a battery bank is crucial and should be accomplished on a regularly scheduled basis. I recommend a bi-weekly schedule – every two weeks, as a minimum. This inspection frequency is essential to help catch harmful battery problems before they become battery "killers!"

Primarily, you should visually inspect for any problems that are actually in plain sight. For example:

- ✓ The general cleanliness of the battery/ies,
- ✓ For any bulging cases,
- ✓ For electrolyte leaks and cracks in the casing,
- ✓ For corrosion at the terminals and other connectors, and
- ✓ Especially for a faulty (loose and/or corroded) connection between the negative battery cable and the chassis (Ground)!!!

(**Comment:** The most common problems that I find are: [1] Corrosion at the terminals and [2] Loose Ground connections. Either one of these will cause poor battery performance. Correct any problem found as soon as possible!)

BATTERY TESTING

Caution: If you try to test the voltage of a battery that just finished charging, you will experience an elevated voltage reading due to a phenomenon known as "**Surface Charge**."

Why does this phenomenon occur? The simplest explanation I can provide is by combining pieces of information from *batteryuniversity.com* and *smartgauge.co.uk*. So, here goes: "Lead-acid batteries are sluggish and cannot convert lead sulfate ($PbSO_4$) to lead and lead dioxide (PbO_2) quickly enough during charge. As a result, most of the charge activity occurs on the surface of the plates, where they are in contact with the electrolyte. It takes some additional time for this chemical reaction to start penetrating deep into the plates. This sluggishness induces a higher state-of-charge on the surface rather than at the inner part of the plate. Therefore, a battery with a surface charge has a slightly elevated voltage reading, rather than an accurate reading."

(**Comment:** An excellent example of surface charge is easily demonstrated by pouring a warm soda [Coke, Pepsi, 7-up, etc. – I prefer Diet Dr. Pepper] straight into a glass of crushed ice. As you have often seen, a foam immediately builds up and gives a false reading about the depth of the beverage in the glass. However, the foam dissipates after some time, and you can eventually see the actual depth.)

"Surface charge is not a battery defect, but a reversible condition resulting from charging." In order to take accurate battery voltage readings, you must normalize any surface charge before testing with your voltmeter. You only have to use <u>one</u> of the following methods to cause a "surface <u>dis</u>charge" and stabilize the condition:

1. Turn "ON" <u>all</u> of your RV's 12-Volt lights (those with incandescent or halogen bulbs draw more current) to remove about 1% of the battery's AH capacity. Leave them all "ON" for at least 10 minutes, then turn "OFF" the lights and wait another 10 minutes before testing.

2. Allow the battery to "rest" for 4 to 12 hours before open-circuit testing.

3. With a battery load tester, apply a heavy load for 15 seconds and wait 10 minutes before testing.

Reminder: Any battery being tested must be disconnected from any load or charger before actual testing. This is referred to as "**Open-Circuit**" testing. (i.e., The battery is disconnected electrically from the RV.) (**Comment:** If you find any reading above 12.7 VDC, your battery[s] is/are **NOT** disconnected! If you see any reading ≥ 13.2 VDC, that means you are directly reading the output of the converter/charger!!)

The best way to test a battery's charge level is to check the specific gravity of the electrolyte. This can be marginally done with an inexpensive hydrometer purchased at any of the auto parts stores. But, if you really want accurate, specific gravity readings, I highly recommend a Portable Battery/Coolant Refractometer with Automatic Temperature Compensation (ATC). (**Comment:** EXTECH Instruments makes the one I've always used – Model RF40. It's not cheap [about $90.00], but if you want accuracy, as well as ease of use, this is the one for you!!)

[source: hardciderhub.com]

Another way to test a battery's charge level is to measure the battery's voltage with a good quality digital multimeter with a display that will show three digits (thousands of a volt DC) to the right of the decimal point for improved accuracy.

Of course, performing both tests increases your overall level of accuracy.

Open-Circuit Test Criteria for both 12-Volt and 6-Volt Batteries:

Open-Circuit Battery Voltage 12V / 6V	Approximate Charge Level	Uncompensated Specific Gravity Range
12.66 / 6.33	100%	1.255 - 1.275
12.47 / 6.24	75% *	1.215 - 1.235
12.28 / 6.14	50% *	1.180 - 1.200
12.08 / 6.04	25% *	1.155 - 1.165
11.81 / 5.91	0% *	1.110 - 1.130

[source: rollsbattery.com]

* Using either the specific gravity or voltage test, if the charge level is BELOW 75%, the battery needs to be recharged **BEFORE** proceeding further.

According to *PacificPowerBatteries.com*'s Battery School, you should **replace a battery** if one or more of the following conditions occur:

"1. If there is a .050 (50/100[ths] [sometimes expressed as 50 "points"]) or more difference in the specific gravity reading between the highest and lowest cell, you have a weak or dead cell(s),"

"2. If the battery will not recharge to a 75% or more charge level."

"3. If a digital voltmeter connected to the battery terminals indicates zero (0) volts, you have an 'open' cell."

"4. If a digital voltmeter indicates 10.45 to 10.65 volts (5.2 to 5.35 volts for a 6-Volt Battery), you probably have a 'shorted' cell. A shorted cell is caused by plates touching, sediment ('mud') build-up, or 'treeing' (lead sulfate crystals grow like tree branches) between the plates."

NOTE: If you have to replace one of the batteries in a battery bank, replace ALL simultaneously. By adding a new battery to an older battery bank, the older batteries will "pull" the new battery down to their level. So don't waste your time and money by just replacing one.

WARNING: Only similar batteries should be connected together in one bank. Do not connect Flooded Lead-Acid, Gel Cell, and AGM batteries together in the same bank. Furthermore, connecting batteries of different sizes or Amp-Hour ratings in the same battery bank is not advisable.

Under-a-Load Charge Level (12-Volt System)

Voltage	Charge Level	Test
12.60+	100%	Open-Circuit
12.06	75%	Under Load
11.58	50%	Under Load
11.04	25%	Under Load
10.5	0%	Under Load

[source: rollsbattery.com]

The table above will benefit most RVers because it demonstrates typical voltage test readings that might be found when testing a battery in use (under a load) rather than open-circuit testing.

BATTERY CONNECTIONS

One situation I run into more often than I should, is a panic call from a customer that has just finished replacing the House Battery Bank. And s/he doesn't "remember where the wires went." So here are a couple of suggestions to help prevent this from happening to you.

1. Before you disconnect any wires or cables from a battery, label them. In the case of a connection cable between two batteries, label both ends of the cable. (**Comment:** I use 1/2" masking tape and a permanent marker. [The bigger the label, the easier to read and the less likely to lose it.] Next, I number the batteries [1,2,3,4], then use capital letters [P for positive, N for negative] for the terminals.

Example: A connector cable between two batteries might be labeled "**1P**" on one end and "**2N**" on the other.)

2. After the labels are attached, draw a diagram showing which end of each wire/cable goes to which terminal on each battery. Keep this drawing for the next time you clean the battery/ies and terminals.

There are three different ways to connect batteries together in a bank:

In a **Series Connection**, batteries of like voltage (typically 6-Volt) and Amp-Hour capacity (nominally 225 AH) are connected to increase the bank's Voltage. The positive terminal of the first battery is connected to the negative terminal of the second battery to reach the desired voltage. The final Voltage is the sum of both batteries' voltage added together while the final Amp-Hours remain unchanged.

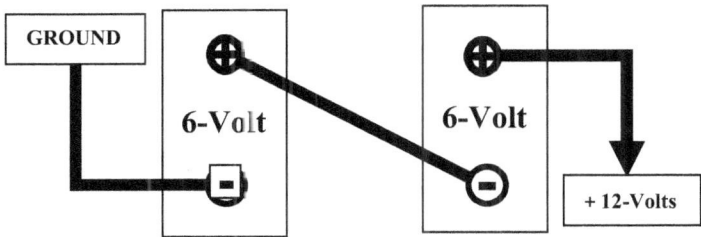

In this example, two 6-Volt Batteries, each rated at 225 Amp-Hours, connected in series, which will result in a 12-Volt bank with a capacity of 225 Amp-Hours. As a result, the bank's Voltage increased while its Amp-Hours remained unchanged.

In the **Parallel Connection**, batteries of like voltages (typically 12-Volts) and Amp-Hour capacities (nominally 100 AH) are connected to increase the Amp-Hour capacity of the bank. The positive terminals of all batteries are connected together, and all negative terminals are connected in the same manner. Thus, the final voltage remains unchanged, while the bank's capacity is the sum of the capacities of the individual batteries of this connection. As a result, Amp-Hours increase while Voltage does not.

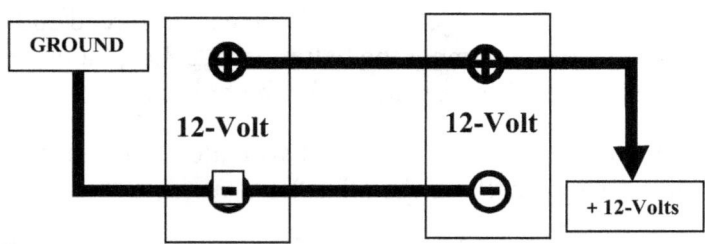

In this example, two 12-Volt Batteries, each rated at 100 Amp-Hours, connected in parallel, will result in a 12-Volt bank with a capacity of 200 Amp-Hours. Thus, the bank's Amp-Hours increased while its Voltage remained unchanged.

A **Series-Parallel Connection** ties two banks of series-connected 6-Volt Batteries (now effectively two 12-Volt Batteries) into a parallel connection. This will give us a total of 12-Volts and 450 Amp-Hours – a great set-up commonly used with inverters.

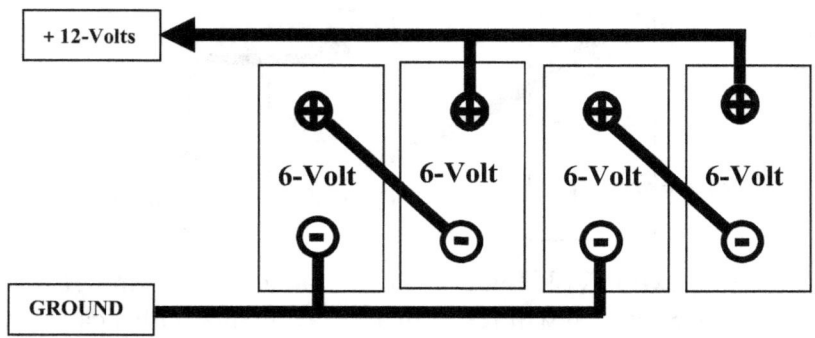

Now, we're going to change direction and deliberately wander into a different "state-of-confusion."

Question: Do you have a "Converter or Inverter"??

Please, don't be embarrassed if you don't know. And, by all means, don't feel like you are alone. Many RVers don't know the difference between the two, let alone which unit they have or how it works.

A **CONVERTER** is an electrical component that "Converts" (changes) 120 Volts of Alternating Current (12 VAC) into 12-Volts of Direct Current (12 VDC). Let's use a simple phrase to help remember what a converter does. Think of it this way:

A <u>C</u>onverter takes 120 V<u>A</u>C and "lowers" it to 12 V<u>D</u>C.

C » A ↓ D   or   CAD for short.

But, here's the real magic of a converter: When a converter is operating, your RV's House Battery Bank is switched out of the system by a relay inside the converter. This relay, which only works when your RV receives 120 VAC power, isolates your House Battery Bank and allows the converter (now think of it as a **"battery substitution device"**) to power everything operating on 12-Volts in the RV. When the RV is disconnected from 120 VAC power, the relay shifts to a different position. Your RV is again operating off your House Battery Bank.

The converter ("battery substitution device") effectively isolates your House Battery Bank from the 12-Volt system but feeds it just enough power to keep it charged up. While a converter is humming away on shore power, something called a "bleeder resistor" inside the unit allows a small amount of the converter's amperage output to be siphoned off to "keep the House Battery Bank fully charged."

Most converters only allow 3 to 5 Amps to "bleed" through to feed the House Battery Bank. This is the primary reason why attempts to recharge a "nearly dead" or "flat" House Battery Bank using an onboard generator take forever or fail miserably.

Nearly dead batteries require somewhere around 30 to 40 Amps of current to recharge quickly. A 3 Amp charge rate would take forever (and usually does). **HINT:** Start your engine and let the alternator recharge your battery bank.

Yes, this works for trailers, too – just make sure you hook the trailer's umbilical cord up to the tow vehicle.

Your RV converter is rated for a specific output amperage, i.e., somewhere between 45 Amps and 80 Amps. If you have a 45 Amp converter, it can only run 45 Amps worth of 12-Volt lights, appliances, and igniter boards in the RV. Also, when this converter is working at its maximum capacity, it is drawing around 5 Amps out of the 30 or 50 Amps available from the campground's 120 Volt electrical supply.

Let's say you're plugged in, and you're using a couple of 12-Volt overhead lights (3 Amps) and a ceiling fan (4 Amps). In this case, your converter is drawing very little from the campground's 120 Volt electrical supply.

But, in another scenario, let's say you're using a lot of 12-Volt incandescent lights (six bulbs alone is 9 Amps – 1.5 Amps per bulb), you're running the furnace fan (11 Amps), water pump (4 Amps), bathroom vent fan (2.5 Amps), range hood fan (2.5 Amps), and the battery is being charged by the converter's charger (3 Amps). When the converter runs close to its total capacity, it will draw a full 5 Amps from the campground's 120 Volt electrical supply. If you are plugged into a 30 Amp outlet, that leaves you with just 25 Amps to run all your other 120 Volt appliances and accessories.

(For more information about RV 120 Volt electricity, please read the ***Primer*** titled, *Understanding Your RV's "SHORE POWER."*)

Hopefully, all of this 12-Volt demand will not be happening at one time. (Remember to turn things "OFF" when not needed.) The bottom line – the converter amp draw will fluctuate depending on the 12-Volt demand placed on it.

The converter's battery charger is designed to keep the House Bat-teries topped off with its trickle or float charge. The problem with older RV converters is that they are set at a fixed voltage range of 13.5 volts.

If your batteries are fully charged, this can be too much for a float charge, and, over time, it will deplete the water level in the battery's cells. This is why it's essential to check the water level in your batteries regularly (I strongly recommend "a minimum occurrence of once a month!"), especially when you have the RV plugged in for extended periods of time (e.g., While wintering down south).

If you have an older converter, you may want to upgrade to a 3-stage charger that can provide a bulk charge, then an absorption charge, and finally, a float charge. Newer RV converters (e.g., W.F.C.O. and Progressive Dynamics converters and W.F.C.O. and Parallax upgrade components for older converters) on the market can charge the batteries this way.

There have been three generations of converters in the RV industry:

1. **Ferroresonace** is a bulky step-down transformer with a loud hum, high heat generation, unreliable DC voltage control, trickle charge only, and variable AC Ripple.

(**AC Ripple** is AC voltage that didn't convert to DC voltage and leaks into the 12 VDC system. Any AC Ripple greater than 6 VAC is very damaging to a 12-Volt circuit board.)

2. **Linear** – much lighter, less hum, built-in fan, reasonable voltage control, still trickle charge only.

3. **Switch Mode** – The latest and the greatest. Excellent voltage control, 3-stage voltage charger for the battery/ies, minimal AC ripple (50mV nominal)

Converter Shortcomings

1. Converters are only capable of supplying their rated amount of power (e.g., 45, 55, 60, or 80 Amps)
2. Older Converters are sloppy about voltage level. When the load is low, the voltage is high, and vice-versa.
3. Batteries are subject to the effects of No. 2 above. The internal bleeder resistor is too crude to regulate voltage.
4. No converter is designed to recharge dead batteries or heavily discharged batteries.
5. Newer converters (with regulated battery chargers) are much kinder to batteries and your RV's electrical components.

By the way – there is no "ON/OFF" switch on a converter. It is always plugged in. So, when you connect to shore power or generator power, it automatically comes "ON."

Here are some "converter" questions I am asked quite frequently:

Question: What causes the lights inside the RV to suddenly get brighter??

Answer: This only occurs with the newer switch-mode converters. When the 3-stage charger shifts into "boost" mode, the DC voltage suddenly increases to around 14.4 volts or higher. The increased difference in the current flow level causes the lights to brighten up. (You probably don't even notice the lights dim down later when the converter goes back into "float" mode.)

Question: How do I know which mode the converter is in??

Answer: There is something called a "Charge Wizard," an option for some newer converters. This device is a small square housing that has a cable fixed internally. The other end of the cable has a quick-connect plug that connects into a small outlet on the converter. . Mounted inside the housing is the exposed tip of a LED. Depending on the state of the LED (On, Blinking Slowly, or Blinking Fast), it indicates the converter's charging mode. This wizard also enables you to change the mode manually. If your converter doesn't have a charge wizard capability, you may try checking the converter output voltage with a voltmeter (see Pages 38 & 39 for voltage values).

Question: What are the two 30 Amp fuses on the outside of the converter "box" for??

Answer: Contrary to popular belief, these fuses are not there to monitor the DC output of the converter. Instead, they protect the converter if "someone" accidentally attaches the battery cables backward – Neg to Pos or vice-versa. It's called reverse battery protection. So before replacing a converter suspected of being inoperative, always check these fuses first!

An **INVERTER** is an electrical component that "Inverts" (a different type of change) 12-Volts of Direct Current (12 VDC) into 120 Volts of Alternating Current (12 VAC) – just the opposite of the converter. Here's another simple phrase to remember what an inverter does:

An Inverter takes 12 V<u>D</u>C and "raises" it to 120 V<u>A</u>C.

I » D ↑ A   or   IDA for short.

Inverters range from simple portable units that plug into your cigarette lighter to larger, hard-wired units that are permanently installed. AC wattage ratings are available from 100 Watts up to 4000 Watts or more. About the only thing that you won't be able to operate with a suitably sized inverter is your air conditioner – the colossal size of the battery bank required makes it impractical. However, most other appliances are fair game (typically attached: the microwave, television(s), and a select number of outlets).

Inverter types: There are three (3) main types of inverters. Square Wave, Modified Sine Wave, and True Sine Wave. Let's look at the differences:

Square Wave

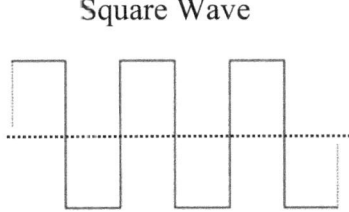

Square Wave inverters are the cheapest. Unfortunately, they are usually the least efficient and will not run any of your sensitive electronic equipment. This is because the AC waveform they produce differs from what you get from the shore or generator. Instead of being a smooth sine wave, it is a square wave. The unit simply changes polarity in abrupt "jolts." These jolts' abrupt drop and rise is alternating current, but the abrupt change results in a "square" waveform. That square waveform causes small, square TV pictures and will not operate some motors or other electric appliances.

Square Wave inverters are usually only adequate for power tools, some motors, and incandescent lights. Definitely not recommended for an RV! In fact, square wave inverters are largely obsolete because the waveform shape is not well suited for running most modern appliances.

Modified Sine Wave

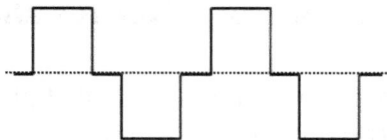

Modified Sine Wave (also referred to as Quasi Sine Wave) inverters are in the middle of the road. They produce an output waveform close to a true sine wave. They will work adequately with most devices, including TVs and computers. You may see some slight distortion lines on the TV or hear a slight buzz on the stereo. Still, for the most part, these inverters provide quite acceptable performance. One noted exception is that most laser printers won't work correctly with a Modified Sine Wave inverter. These inverters are also middle-of-the-road as far as cost goes, too.

True Sine Wave

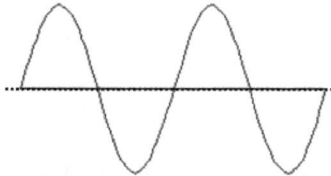

True Sine Wave inverters are precisely that. They produce a practically perfect sine wave output. These units will operate even the fussiest electronic device. Still, they are much more expensive than their cousins, the Modified Sine Wave inverters. Do you need one? Yes. Especially if you are upgrading the equipment in an older RV to today's highly sensitive pieces of equipment.

How an Inverter/Charge Works. All Inverter/Chargers have two modes of operation, but only function in one mode at a time (never both at the same time:

Standby / Idle Mode. When you <u>are</u> plugged into shore power or running your generator, the inverter receives its power from the RV's power distribution panel (120 VAC) – usually via its own 30 Amp circuit breaker – and only operates as a converter that changes the 120 VAC to 12 VDC and recharges the battery/ies.

Here's what's happening: When the inverter recognizes receiving shore power or generator power, an internal automatic transfer relay (switch) closes, and the power quickly and efficiently passes <u>through</u> the inverter to the attached appliances. <u>No inverting occurs.</u>

(**Comment:** However, the input 120 VAC is shared between the Charger and the Loads. That means the charger's amp draw will be part of the maximum allowed 30 Amp flow and could lead to an unexpectedly popped circuit breaker. Remember to factor this into the total amp draw when turning on appliances powered through the inverter.)

Inverter Mode. When you are <u>not</u> plugged into shore power and <u>not</u> running your generator, the inverter draws 12 VDC power from the "House" Battery Bank. Then, it uses inversion magic to provide 120 VAC power to the electrical appliances (a.k.a. "AC Loads") connected to the inverter's output.

(**Comment:** Sorry to say so, but contrary to popular belief, when the inverter is working on battery power, it does <u>not</u> run its "charger" side to recharge the batteries. [A "perpetual" machine it is not!])

In a Nutshell: Depending on the presence of "shore or generator" 120 VAC power, the internal Automatic Transfer Relay switches between the Standby/Idle Mode and the Inverter Mode. If "shore or generator" 120 VAC is present, the unit will only be a battery charger, and the incoming 120 VAC will "pass" right through to the attached appliances. If the "shore or generator" 120 VAC power stops for any reason, the unit immediately becomes an inverter. It continues to provide 120 VAC power to any attached appliances that were previously operating.

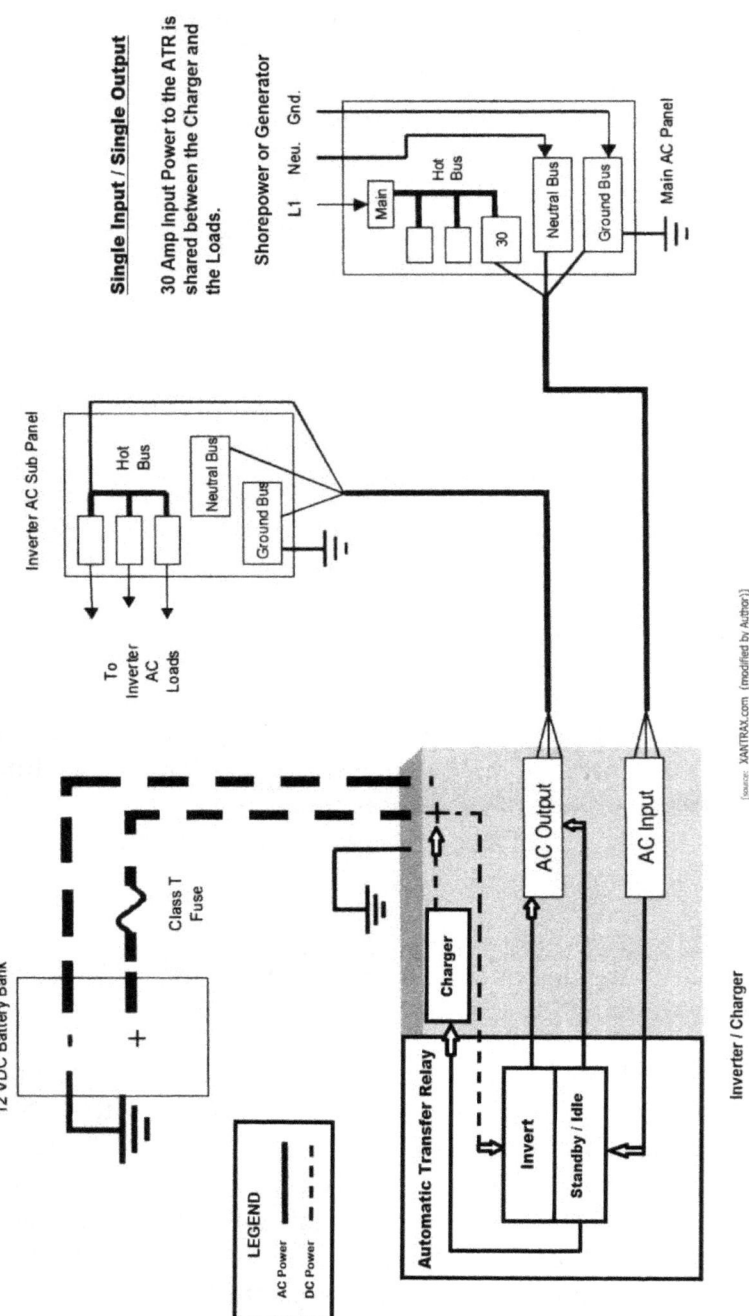

Inverter Battery Charging. Many of the inverters designed for RV use also have high-quality battery chargers built-in. But, here's a shocker – the charger is a converter! (However, you may be able to turn this unit "OFF.")

(**Comment:** Then why do we call it a charger? Because most RV owners don't know the difference between a converter and an inverter. Since the term "inverter/converter" would add to the confusion ["Which is it?"], the RV industry refers to it as an inverter/charger. You do not have a separate converter if you have an inverter/charger because the converter [charger] is already built into the inverter. It functions just the same as a stand-alone converter. [How's that for stirring up the pot?!])

Most of the major inverter manufacturers provide 3-stage charging as standard equipment in their inverters. These chargers typically can deliver from 25 to 150 Amps of charge current and run very well with generator power, allowing you to quickly recharge your battery/ies while dry camping (boondocking). These 3-stage chargers are not supposed to boil the water out of your battery/ies. Instead, they will bring them to full charge and then taper back to a valid float charge – these units can safely be left plugged in continuously. **NOTE:** If your battery/ies is/are boiling over, there is probably a problem with the charger side of the inverter.

Inverter Input – The inverter receives 120 VAC power from the post or generator via the master circuit breaker panel inside the RV. An internal transfer switch allows the 120 VAC power to "pass through" the inverter to an output sub-panel. A small amount of the incoming power is routed to the charger for battery maintenance.

When 120 VAC power is unavailable, the inverter receives 12 VDC power from the House Battery Bank. It takes the DC input and runs it into a pair (or more) of power switching transistors. By rapidly turning these transistors on and off and feeding opposite sides of a transformer, it makes the transformer think it is getting AC. The transformer changes this 12-Volt "Alternating" Current into 120 VAC at the output. Depending on the quality and complexity of the inverter, it may put out one of the three "sine waves" discussed earlier.

Inverter Output – The output is usually routed to a power distribution sub-panel with its own circuit breakers. These breakers protect the wiring to your microwave, TVs, and other equipment connected to outlets powered by the inverter.

Inverter/Charger — Input/Output Configurations

Single Input / Single Output

Single Input / Dual Output

Dual Input / Dual Output

You will have to check your owner's manual to ascertain which configuration applies to your inverter. The configuration you have will determine how many, which type, and the rating of the circuit breakers your inverter may have.

Inverter Circuit Breakers – Most inverters have several built-in circuit breakers.

There is usually a 30 Amp circuit breaker on the input side in the RV's master circuit breaker panel. This breaker prevents the inverter from drawing too much power from the 120 VAC system.

On the output side, there may be two (2) switch-type or push-button circuit breakers. One rated at 20 Amps and the other rated at 15 Amps or both rated at 20 Amps. (Although, I have seen some inverters with just one 25 or one 30 Amp breaker.) These breakers prevent the loads from over-drawing too much power from/through the inverter.

(**Comment:** If there is no power available to "half" of your RV and that half is usually powered by or through the inverter, check the inverter's circuit breaker[s]. It's a good possibility that one or more may have "popped.")

If you have an inverter, you probably have a ton of questions.

Because there are so many different models, set-ups, and output configurations, it will be virtually impossible to answer all of them in this simple *Primer*. However, here is an answer to the most common question: *Should I always leave my inverter in the "ON" position?*

Answer: **YES**, when the RV is in use, you want the inverter to respond to a demand (power something up), and you don't have, or lost, shore power or generator power. **NO**, when the RV is in storage (i.e., not in normal use). Turn it "OFF" if you don't want the inverter to respond to any demand. (p.s. You should also turn "OFF" all attached electrical appliances. And don't forget about the Automatic Generator Start [AGS] if you have one.) Read your owner's manual for specific information concerning the storage of your inverter.

Remember: Whether the inverter is turned "ON" or "OFF," shore power will always pass through its internal transfer switch to power all the attached equipments. That means when you are connected to shore power or running a generator, the inverter will not invert 12 VDC to 120 VAC, even if the inverter is "ON."

If you are dry camping, the inverter only responds to a demand for power – something has to be turned on to cause the inverter to work. It does not automatically provide 120 VAC if an attached piece of equipment is not turned on. If it did, your battery bank would run down quite quickly. Some inverters have the capability of setting the minimum demand level, e.g., they can be set to respond to a coffee maker but not to an electric clock or cell phone charger plugged into one of the inverter output outlets.

(**Comment:** My best recommendation for all inverter owners – In order to become an efficient inverter user, you must read the owner's manual very carefully and thoroughly. Don't get bogged down if you don't understand something. Keep reading! Sometimes things are explained more clearly a little later in the manual. For example, suppose you figure out for yourself how to set up and operate your inverter. In that case, the knowledge will stay with you much longer than if someone casually tries to tell you.

AMP-HOURS

This subject is all-important to every inverter owner, be they casual users or serious boondockers.

As stated earlier in this ***Primer***, a Deep-Cycle Battery's power capability is rated in Amp-Hours. The Amp-Hour rating is based on the standard of a 20-hour discharge cycle. (e.g., A 100 Amp-Hour battery can deliver 5 Amps of current for 20 hours.)

However, that same battery can't supply 100 Amps for 1 hour. It can only supply 100 Amps for about 1/2 an hour. In fact, if the load is increased to 100 Amps, the battery will only have about 45 Amp-Hours available at this level of discharge.

Wow, how does that work? Here's my analogy – A battery bank is like your savings account. Suppose you take your money out slowly, in small amounts. In that case, the remainder can still work for you (earn interest), and the money will obviously last longer. However, suppose you take large sums of cash out too often. In that case, the remainder can't earn you any interest to speak of, and pretty soon, your account is totally "flat."

Let's take this analogy a little further. We can say that your House Battery Bank is your savings account, and you have a certain amount of Amp-Hours "deposited" into it. To ensure this "account" will last as long as possible, you need to ensure you don't take any amount out that is too extensive. You will need to be aware of what kind of "withdrawals" you will be making to do this. This "withdrawal" process is called your "**discharge rate**."

When you are dry camping (no generator running or shore power), there are two types of discharge rates you need to pay attention to:

One for 12-Volt Devices and one for 120 Volt Appliances.

Starting with the 12 VDC devices, let's look at some DC amp draws.

DC CURRENT USAGE CHART*

Device	DC Amps
Fluorescent light, double, 30W	2.0
Fluorescent light, single, 8 W	0.7
Fluorescent light, double, 8W	1.3
Fluorescent light, single, 15 W	1.2
Fluorescent light, double, 15W	2.5
Incandescent light, single 1141 bulb	1.5
Incandescent light, double, 1141 bulb	3.0
Incandescent light, single, 1003 bulb	1.0
Incandescent light, double, 1003 bulb	2.0

TV Antenna Booster	0.2
Digital Satellite Receiver (crank-up – automatic)	2.0-5.0
Refrigerator on LP mode (over/under – side by side)	0.5-1.0
Fan Motor, 500 CFM – low speed	1.3
Fan Motor, 700 CFM – med speed	2.6
Fan Motor, 1000 CFM – hi speed	5.5
Furnace Fan Motor	8.0-11.0
Roof Vent Fan - bathroom	2.5
Water Pump (depending on G.P.M. flow rate)	4.5-6.0

[source: rv-boondocking-adventure.com]

* NOTE: The DC usage ratings above are approximate. For a more accurate calculation, check the amp draw on each 12 VDC device in your RV.

With a 12-VDC powered device, figuring out the discharge rate in Amp-Hours is very simple. All you have to do is multiply the amperage of the device by the number of hours you plan to use it or have used it.

For example, say you want to run your Fan-Tastic Vent fan to cool off the inside of the RV from noon to 4 p.m. If you use the medium speed setting, that "pulls" about 2.6 Amps. So, 2.6 Amps × 4 hours = a discharge of 10.4 Amp-Hours. Pretty straightforward, wouldn't you say?

Now, it's time to take a look at some 120 VAC appliance wattages and/or amp draws.

Each AC appliance has a "rating" label attached to it somewhere. This label will identify either the wattage or amp draw of the appliance. If the amperage is listed, use that number. If the wattage is listed, divide that value by 120 to get the amperage rating.

(A Law of Physics: Amps × Volts = Watts. For more in-depth information about how this electrical concept works, please read the **Primer** titled, *Understanding Your RV's "SHORE POWER."*)

To continue our discussion on computing discharge rate, let's say you want to run your HD TV off the inverter while stopping at a rest area for lunch. The TV is probably rated at 200 watts. Divide the 200 watts by 120 volts, and you get 1.67 AC Amps. (watts ÷ volts = amps).

To further convert AC (120 Volt) appliance amperage into DC Amp-Hours, you need to add one more step to the calculation process. Simply multiply the AC amperage by a constant AC to DC conversion factor of 10.

So, you multiply the 1.67 AC Amps by 10, and you now get 16.70 DC Amps. Thus, if you limit your TV watching to 30 minutes, you will only withdraw 8.35 DC Amp-Hours from your battery bank. (A calculation table representing this mathematical sequence follows. This table also has additional spaces for you to demonstrate your arithmetic prowess as well.)

Determining DC Amp-Hours used by AC Appliances

Item	Watts	÷ Volts	= AC Amps	AC to DC Conversion Factor	= DC Amps		Hrs. Per Day	= DC Amp-Hours
HD TV	200	120	1.67	X 10	16.70	X	.5	8.35
		120		X 10		X		
		120		X 10		X		
		120		X 10		X		
		120		X 10		X		

Typical Power Consumption

The chart identifies typical power consumption for common AC loads. Use it as a guide to help identify your DC Amp-Hour discharges.

Appliance	Typical Wattage	DC Amps X Appliance Run Times = DC Amp-Hours						
		5 Min.	15 Min.	30 Min.	1 Hr.	2 Hr.	3 Hr.	24 Hr.
VCR/DVD	50	.35	1.04	2.09	4.17	8.34	12.51	
Lamp	100	.69	2.08	4.15	8.30	16.6	24.90	199.20
HD TV	200	1.39	4.18	8.35	16.70	33.40	50.10	
Blender	300	2.08	6.25	12.5				
3/8 Drill	500	3.46	10.43	20.85				
RV Refrigerator	750				20.63	41.25	61.88	495*
Toaster	1000	6.91	20.83	41.65				
Vacuum	1100	7.61	22.93	45.85	91.70			
Coffee maker	1200	8.30	25.00	50.00				
Microwave	1500	10.38	31.25	62.50	125	250	375	#
Hair Dryer	1865	12.90	38.85	77.70	155			
Convection Oven	2400	16.60	50	100	200	400	600	#

[source: xantrex.com & modified by Author]

* — Calculated as operating for only 20 minutes out of every hour (no refrigerator works 100% of the time – it cycles on and off). Even so, this 24 hour, high Amp-Hour discharge is why RV (an absorption system capable of using LP gas or electric) refrigerators are not customarily hooked up to an inverter (**Comment:** If yours is connected to an inverter, I sincerely recommend shifting to LP mode or run the generator while dry camping.) **Note:** Residential (electric only) refrigerators usually have an independent two-battery bank and a separate (dedicated) inverter.

— Obviously, if the microwave or convection oven will be used for any length of time (i.e., > 10 minutes), you should consider starting the generator instead!

Your inverter's **efficiency loss** is also important to consider if you are serious about monitoring your actual Amp-Hour discharge rate.

Most inverters are only 80% or 90% efficient. The efficiency rating of an inverter is usually documented in the inverter's owner's manual.

This efficiency loss means that if your inverter is 90% efficient and your appliance requires 1 Amp, the inverter actually needs to draw an extra 10% from the battery bank to make up for the efficiency loss. So, in reality, your inverter is drawing 1.1 Amps for every 1 Amp that it is supplying to the load. If your inverter is only 80% efficient, it must draw 1.2 Amps from the bank for each amp it provides. (**Comment:** If your inverter is less than 80% efficient, please consider replacing it with a new one!!)

Since only the AC appliance discharge rates are funneled through the inverter, you will have to add 10% to your DC Amp-Hours total in order to account for the 10% efficiency loss (assuming your inverter is 90% efficient). For example, our HD TV's Amp-Hour discharge for 30 minutes was 8.35. So, 8.35 × 1.1 = 9.19 corrected DC Amp-Hours.

Your, now, total Amp-Hour discharge rate is the sum of the DC Amp-Hours plus the efficiency loss correction factor. **But**, there is still one other dynamic that you need to account for. And that is the energy that is lost due to the resistance of the wiring and battery/ies. Since all of the devices and appliances use wires, this factor applies to all of the calculations. So, if you take your total Amp-Hours and add a recommended 5% adjustment for the **resistance factor**, you will finally have your Amp-Hour discharge rate <u>grand</u> total.

The Collective Amp-Hour Consumption Formulas

(In all formulas, 1.1 is the correction factor for 90% inverter efficiency.)

(AC Amps × 10) × 1.1 × Hrs. of Operation + 5% = DC Amp-Hours
(Watts ÷ 12 VDC) × 1.1 × Hrs. of Operation + 5% = DC Amp-Hours
(AC V × A ÷ 12 VDC) × 1.1 × Hrs. of Operation + 5% = DC Amp-Hours

[source: **Error! Bookmark not defined.**xantrex.com.]

Here's a quick scenario to illustrate the whole concept –

When you stopped at noon to take a half-hour lunch break, you turned on the TV, made a quick pot of coffee, used the toaster for your tuna on toast sandwiches, and ran the Fan-Tastic vent on high for air circulation. And here's how the Amp-Hours stacked up:

Item	Efficiency Corrected Amp-Hours	Resistance Factor Adjustment	Total Consumption
HD TV	9.19	0.46	9.65
Coffee Maker	50.00	2.50	52.50
Toaster	21.00	1.05	22.05
Fan – Hi-speed (a 12 VDC Appliance)	Not Applicable*	0.14	2.89
* The fan's operating voltage does not funnel through the inverter. It comes directly from the battery bank – 2.75 DC Amps.			87.09

"But wait! There's more..." If you have a "typical" four 6-Volt battery bank connected in series/parallel, you have approximately 450 Amp-Hours of total storage capacity. (***Please remember:*** Deep-Cycle Batteries are designed to be discharged no more than 80% before permanent damage occurs [0.80 × 450 = 360]. However, 50% cycling is considered to be prudent in order to provide a much longer battery life. So you only have 225 Amp-Hours of "safe" energy to draw on (0.50 × 450 = 225).

Your lunch break consumed 87.09 DC Amp-Hours. If you subtract that figure from the "safe" value of 225 Amp-Hours, you have a result of 137.91 Amp-Hours remaining before you need to recharge the battery bank.

Fortunately, you will probably continue to drive your motorhome for a few more hours before you stop for the night. And, "Oh Golly!" there's still one more thing to make you aware of – for best charging, always plan on using the inverter's charger to recharge your battery bank. That means using shore power or generator power to provide 120 VAC to the inverter/charger. Why? Because the alternator attached to your engine will typically provide only a charge level of about 85% of full charge. (That's because it's only a Bulk Charger!)

Okay…this section is finally finished!! Whew. Hopefully, it hasn't scared you away from dry camping and successful inverter use. It was only intended to make you aware of the many different concepts associated with successful inverter use. Suppose you aren't aware of everything that is involved. In that case, you could quite possibly be investing in a new battery bank much sooner (and probably more often) than necessary. And, as you know, that's expensive.

Now let's talk about the **Battery Disconnect System**.

Today, most RV owners are quickly introduced to this system. The switch(s) for the battery disconnect system is/are commonly located just inside the RV's door, while some are actually in the battery compartment. The battery disconnect comprises either 1 or 2 electronic or manual switch(s) – usually 1 for trailers and 2 for motorhomes. The switch(s) is/are turned to disconnect the battery system. The battery disconnect switches on a motorhome are a very small part of the complete battery control center (more about this later).

The solenoid pictured here (referred to as a "**battery disconnect relay**") is used to disconnect the battery/ies during periods of storage (don't want the battery/ies to run down from phantom or parasitic loads) or when the RV is being serviced. **Note:** The picture above is oriented "right side up" so we can read the printing on the label. When this unit is installed, it is usually mounted "upside down."

(**Comment:** The "heart" of this unit is a unique latching relay explicitly developed for RV use. While this relay can carry heavy current loads, it requires NO power to stay open or closed. Instead, it only draws power during activation [being opened or closed].)

WARNING: Don't try replacing this unit with a "plain" 4-post solenoid. IT WON'T WORK!

The disconnect relay operates by applying 12 VDC to the solenoid coil in one of two directions:

1. To open the relay and disconnect the battery bank from the system, +12 VDC is applied to the "S" terminal (labeled Brown/Gray in the picture), and Ground (−12 VDC) is applied to the "I" terminal (labeled White/Purple in the picture).

2. To close the relay and connect the battery bank to the system, +12 VDC is applied to the "I" terminal, and Ground (−12 VDC) is applied to the "S" terminal.

The +12 VDC comes via the disconnect switches mounted in the RV and is routed to the relays in the "box." (**NOTE:** On the electronic disconnect system, the switches are "momentary" switches. Their normal position is in the middle. You "rock" the switch UP to close the relay and DOWN to open the relay. When you release the switch, it returns to the middle position.)

Okay, time to change the subject a little bit more. Let's talk about something that causes a lot of headache and heartache for many motorhome owners – The mysterious **Battery Control Center**.

(**Comment:** The first time I ran across one of these was in 1973, when my Dad bought his first motorhome, a 26 ft. GMC. The coach manuals didn't cover the battery control system, so Dad asked me to trace it out and diagram it so we could decipher how it worked. Compared to today's battery control centers, the '73 version was very rudimentary, albeit effective.)

According to Intellitec's service manual, "The battery control center is a centralized power switching, fusing, and distribution center. Power from the main (a.k.a. "chassis") and the auxiliary (a.k.a. "house") battery/ies is fed through the battery control center. The full power of both batteries is available within the "box." The system consists of two (2) battery disconnect relays, a bi-directional battery charging circuit, an auxiliary (a.k.a. "boost") start function to provide a "jump-start" from the auxiliary battery, and ignition power switching relay circuit."

(BTW – Intellitec is the leading manufacturer of electronic controls for RVs. All of their manuals can be found at *www.intellitec.com*)

The battery control center in a motorhome can be located almost anywhere. Typically, in a "gas" motorhome, the "box" is located in the engine compartment. In a "diesel" motorhome, the favorite locations seem to be either in a basement compartment on the driver's side, right below the driver's side window, or in the compartment where the shore power enters the coach. Without question, it is a Christopher Columbus ("seek and ye shall find") location – well hidden in some RVs.

Here's what to look for, so you'll know it when you see it. Almost all motorhome battery control centers contain three (3) solenoids used (and referred to) as relays. Two are identical, but the other is unique.

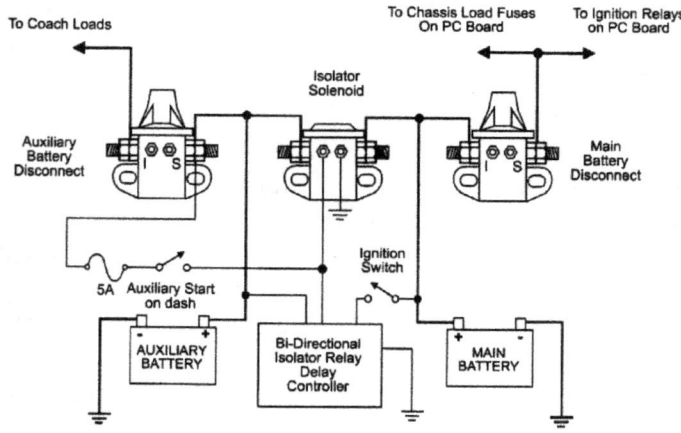

Battery Control System
[source: intellitec.com]

(**Comment:** Since some OEMs construct their units without one, there may be quite a few motorhomes out "there" that do not have a battery disconnect solenoid for the Chassis [Main] battery. Resultantly, the Chassis battery self-discharges over time. Why? Because the Chassis battery does not receive a charge from the converter/charger, only from the engine's alternator. The affected motorhome owners typically hook up a 3-Stage, external battery charger to the chassis battery to keep it from going "flat" when in storage or when the RV is lived in but not driven frequently.)

Sometimes these solenoids are located behind a printed circuit board with many fuses (ATO – blade type) mounted onto it. (**Comment**: These fuses protect many 12-Volt systems throughout the RV. If something powered by 12 VDC isn't working and a fuse cannot be found on the main fuse panel or the ignition circuit board, try looking for an associated fuse on this board. I strongly recommend you find and scrutinize this particular board carefully, so you know just which equipments are powered and fused through it.)

The unique solenoid pictured in the diagram on the previous page, and below is the **isolator solenoid**. It is used to connect the two (chassis and house) battery banks together for charging.

This solenoid (a "plain" 4-post solenoid) and a "little BIRD" (**B**i-directional **I**solator **R**elay **D**elay) Controller are the significant components of the charging circuit.

According to Intellitec's manual, "the BIRD will charge both battery banks if either battery/bank is being charged. The charging circuit operates by sensing the voltage on the chassis and House Battery banks. For example, suppose either bank's voltage exceeds 13.3 volts (the minimum necessary to charge a battery) for more than one minute. In that case, the isolator solenoid will engage, thus tying both battery/banks together and charging both.

"When the engine is running, and the voltage drops below 12-Volts for more than one minute, the isolator solenoid will open, thus directing the entire alternator output solely to the chassis functions.

"If the ignition is "OFF" and the House Battery voltage drops below 12.8 volts for one minute, the isolator solenoid will open, thus preventing the house loads from discharging the Chassis Battery." (Nice safety feature, wouldn't you say.)

Should the chassis bank not have sufficient charge to start the engine, the **auxiliary (or boost) start** function temporarily provides a "jump-start" from the House Battery Bank to the Chassis Battery Bank. Just like using "jumper" cables to connect from one vehicle's battery to another vehicle's battery, the isolator solenoid makes the connection between the two battery banks. This "jumper" function is accomplished by pressing the appropriate dash-mounted switch. (Make sure you know where it is located.)

By now, you have figured out that if one or more of these special solenoids fail, you are going to have some serious 12-Volt issues. And, my friends, they do, occasionally, fail. So, before you change out either of your battery banks, make sure you have the solenoids tested for proper function.

And, for our last topic – **Winter or Long Term Storage**

Most RVs constructed are stored for long periods of time, especially during the winter months. This storage can be very hard on your battery/ies if you don't take care of them.

Battery/ies in storage self-discharge over time. This is a natural phenomenon and will cause your battery/ies to slowly go "flat." However, deep discharges drastically shorten your battery/ies' life.

Extremely cold temperatures can cause your battery/ies to freeze if they aren't adequately charged (Remember, the electrolyte is 65% water in a fully charged battery and more in a discharged battery.) A battery close to fully charged is far more resistant to freezing than a partially charged battery. Freezing will generally kill a flooded cell battery. Some of the gel batteries and most of the AGM-type batteries are more resistant to damage from freezing, but it's better to prevent it.

To avoid all this potential mayhem, some charging current will have to be applied to the battery/ies periodically during the storage period.

To keep your battery/ies safe through a winter storage period, consider removing and storing them in a warmer place, like a garage. Then, check the voltage once a month and do an overnight recharge if the "open circuit" voltage falls to the 80% charge level point. (See the chart on Page 9.)

If removing the battery/ies just isn't possible, then there are several things that you must do when the RV is put into storage.

1. Ensure that ALL electrical loads are disconnected from your House Battery/ies. There are lots of things in your RV that may put a tiny load on your battery/ies even though everything is "OFF." For example, most TV antennas and propane (LP) detectors are small drains on the battery/ies. Also, suppose the current draw is only a few milliamps. In that case, these "phantom or parasitic loads" will run your battery/ies down over time! Your best bet is to identify which 12-Volt fuses protect these units and temporarily remove them. It is a real good idea to check the battery with an ammeter to ensure no current drain.

2. (**Comment:** And, don't forget to reinstall the fuses when you take the RV out of storage! I label each fuse, place them in a zip lock bag, and tape the bag to the inside of the RV's entry door. That way, I can't forget about the fuses because I see them in the bag every time I open the door.)

3. Provide for some sort of charging to offset the battery's tendency to self-discharge. It is best to let the battery/ies discharge slightly over a few weeks or a month and, then, do a full recharge overnight. **CAUTION:** Trickle chargers and unregulated solar panels can slowly boil off electrolyte, or worse, fail to maintain the charge, allowing your battery/ies to become deeply discharged. If your RV has an older model converter, **do not** leave it plugged in constantly to keep your batteries up! That converter will boil your battery/ies **DRY** in a big hurry! If you must leave your RV plugged into AC power over the storage period, make sure to either unplug the converter or switch it off at the RV's circuit breaker panel. It's far better to run the converter overnight every 3 or 4 weeks or so, as needed, to charge the battery/ies. Another possibility would be to put the converter on a simple plug-in timer and set it to be "ON" for about 1 hour a day. If you have a smart 3-stage charger, it may be safe to leave it plugged in at all times; however, you should pay very close attention to the electrolyte level in the battery/ies as an insurance policy. As noted before, boiling a battery down to where

the plates are exposed to air will cause permanent damage to the battery. Don't let this happen to you!

4. Check on the battery/ies from time to time during the storage period. Stop by at least once a month and check battery voltage and electrolyte levels. Don't walk away from your RV battery/ies in November and expect them to be still ready to go in May. Folks who adopt the "Out-of-Sight, Out-of-Mind" approach to battery maintenance are usually the ones buying a new set of batteries at the start of every RVing season!

SUGGESTION for motorhome owners: When your motorhome is in storage, it is a good idea to visit it at least once a month. (Sunday afternoon always worked for me.) Plan on staying for a while because several things need to be done.

Before you leave the house, gather a few things you will need: the newspaper, that new book you started, or even the latest DVD you've wanted to watch. You may also want to pack or pick up something to eat and drink. Finally, if it's cold outside, take along a couple of electric space heaters if you don't have heat pumps in the RV.

Once you get to the RV, do a walk around first. Ensure the tires are still inflated, nothing has come loose or broken off, and, heaven forbid, nothing has been broken into or removed.

The second thing you want to do is check the water level in the battery/ies. **WARNING:** If the battery/ies has/have ice inside any of the cells – STOP! Never attempt to charge a battery with ice in it. The battery/ies will probably have to be replaced.

Then, enter the RV.

Start the generator. That's a good way of determining if your House Batteries have a charge. Low or dead batteries will not start a generator. (If they don't start the generator, you may have to take the battery/ies home (or to a battery shop) to service and charge them.)

Ensure you put a good electrical load on the generator – heat pumps, space heaters, or air conditioners. It needs an electrical load in order to heat up and dry out the windings (a.k.a. "exercising the generator");

otherwise, you are just running the engine side of the generator – not very productive.

Next (or if the battery/ies are too low to start the generator), start the propulsion engine. Move the RV forward and backward (about 30 yards in each direction if possible) to operate the brakes and transmission a couple of times. Don't worry about retracting the leveling jacks – you should <u>not</u> have lowered the hydraulic leveling jacks down when you put your motorhome in storage. WHY NOT? Because, eventually, they'll leak, or worse, after a while, they'll get "stuck" in position, and you'll have a devil of a time getting them to retract in the Spring. Also, when the leveling jacks are down for an extended period of time in a moisture-laden climate (rain or snow), little rust "scabs" can occur on the piston (the shiny part). These scabs stick out from the cylinder's surface and prevent it from retracting – more about this in a future ***Primer***.

If necessary, run the propulsion engine until the House Battery/ies has/have enough charge to start the generator. Then, run the generator long enough to bring the House Battery/ies to full charge. (***Remember:*** <u>After</u> the battery/ies is/are fully charged, you can add distilled water to the battery/ies, if necessary – preferably with a battery fill system.) This should not have to be done more than once a month – maybe less (assuming you have a well-maintained battery/ies).

While the battery/ies are charging, crank up the TV antenna and tune in your favorite sports event. Sit back and relax.

After the appropriate amount of time, you're ready to shut everything down and put the RV back into a state of hibernation. (Don't forget to turn off the amplifier to the antenna.) Finally, the battery bank has been charged, the RV generator has been exercised, and you've had some alone time. Now that's a win-win situation for you and your RV.

Here's a Quick Re-Cap of this *Primer's* lessons:

The 12-Volt Electrical System is the "Lifeblood" of any RV!!

A 12-Volt Battery is <u>not</u>, repeat <u>NOT</u>, just a 12-Volt Battery!

Batteries are simple chemical-electrical wonders.

You cannot ignore the battery/ies in your RV!

There is no such thing as a "Maintenance Free" battery
ALL batteries require maintenance, and most require "watering."

A "Chassis" Battery Bank provides power to the engine.

A "House" Battery Bank provides power to everything requiring 12-Volts in the RV, including starting the generator.

All of the circuit boards that control appliances and/or generate ignition are powered by 12-Volts in an RV, especially the Refrigerator, Furnace(s), Water Heater, and rooftop Air Conditioner(s).

(For more information about the RV appliances, please read the *Primer* titled *Understanding Your RV's "APPLIANCES."*)

The LP Alarm, TV Antenna, TV Satellite Dish, and most lights (including fluorescents) are all devices powered by 12-Volts.

There is only a range of $85/100^{ths}$ of a volt between a fully charged and fully discharged battery.

There is a **BIG** difference between Open-Circuit Testing and Under-a-Load Testing of a battery.

A Surface Charge <u>WILL</u> give you a false voltage reading.

Where to look for 12-Volt Fuses: <u>AT</u> the Main 12-Volt Fuse Panel, <u>ON</u> the Ignition Control Panel and <u>IN</u> the Battery Control Center.

The Converter uses 120 VAC to make 12 VDC.

A Converter is also a "battery substitution device."

The Inverter uses 12 VDC to make 120 VDC.

An Inverter's Charger is really a Converter.

Battery Discharge Rate is very important.

The Battery Disconnect System and/or the Battery Control Center are important enough that you need to know where they are located and how they work.

When was the last time you "watered" your House Battery/ies?

And, please, remember this as long as you own an RV - -

"Most RV 'House' batteries do not die from old age; they are <u>annihilated</u>, in their prime, by neglect!"

Well, with that last thought-provoking statement, I'll say that we have finished your primer on the 12-Volt RV "BATTERY POWER." Hopefully, this book has encouraged you to seek answers to more complicated electrical questions. That's great!! And, more so, this book has caused you to view RV electricity from a different direction. That's FANTASTIC!!

Since you now have a good handle on the basics, you are, indeed, ready to move on to a more advanced state of knowledge about your RV's 12 VDC electrical system. At this point, it is time to do the unthinkable. Yep, you guessed it – it's time to read your entire collection of the manufacturer's 12-Volt equipment operating manuals/instructions. Enjoy!

Thank you for reading this *Primer*.

May you always be a

"12-Volt Savvy,

Battery Maintaining,

and Safety Conscious RVer"!!

Sincerely,

Dale

A Veteran Owned and Operated Company
"Non Sibi Sed Patriae"

INDEX

TOPICS

	Page
Battery	
12-Volt Battery	10
3-Stage Charger	38
Acceptance/Absorption Charge	38
Adding Water	20
Absorbed Glass Matte (AGM)	34
Analogy	11
Automotive	32
Bulk Charge	38
Cell	14
Charging	38
Charging Path	15
Chassis	31
Connections	45
Deep-Cycle	32
Discharging Path	18
Float Charge	39
Freshness	37
Gassing	16
Gel Cell	34
House	31
How to Add Water	28
How to Clean Terminals	26
Inspection	41
Lithium Ferro Phosphate (LFP)	35
Lead-Acid (Flooded)	12
On-Board Watering System	29
Open-Circuit Testing	43
Plates	13
Rating	36
Replacing	43
RV/Marine	33
Solar Battery Charging	23
Separator	14
Servicing	24
Sulfation	21
Sulfation Prevention	22

	Page
Battery (continued)	
Surface charge	41
Ten Commandments	40
Terminal Corrosion	25
Testing	41
Under-a-Load Testing	44
Winter or Long Term Storage	68
Battery Control Center	65
Auxilary (Boost) Start	68
Isolator Solenoid	67
Battery Disconnect System	64
Disconnect Relay	64
Converter	47
AC Ripple	49
Battery Substitution Device	47
Ferroresonace	49
Linear	49
Shortcomings	49
Switch Mode	49
Inverter	51
Amp-Hours	57
Battery Charging	55
Calculating DC Amp-Hours	60
Circuit Breakers	56
Converting AC Amps to DC Amps	60
Discharge Rate	58
Efficiency Loss	61
Input	55
Modified Sine Wave	52
Output	56
Resistance Factor	62
Square Wave	51
True Sine Wave	52

	Page
Recap of Lessons	72

CHARTS AND DIAGRAMS

	Page
3-Stage Charging	39
Amp-Hour Consumption Formulas	62
Battery Charging Path	15
Battery Control System	66
Battery Discharging Path	18
DC Current Usage Chart	58
Determining Amp-Hours used by AC Appliances	60
Inverter/Charger System	54
Open Circuit Test Criteria	43
Parallel Connection	46
Series Connection	45
Series/Parallel Connection	46
Typical Power Consumption Chart	60
Under-a-Load Charge Level	44

About Dale, the RV Tech, Teacher, & Author . . .

Dale Lee Sumner is a retired RVIA/RVDA Master Certified RV Service Technician and former owner/president of Mobile RV Medic, Inc.

He has sixty years of experience using and living in RVs (including more than a decade of recent "full-time" RVing) and conducting the business of repairing RVs. Now, he is concentrating on educating the RV owners.

And...Dale loves to teach what he writes! His goal is to provide as many RVers as possible – be they initially "Considering" RVing, just "Beginning" to RV, been "Camping" for years, or are living the dream of "Full-Timing" – with a solid, baseline understanding of the different (non-house-like) functional areas in their RVs.

Dale's teaching style is educational yet casual and entertaining. He writes in a down-to-earth, non-technical fashion so every reader can quickly become familiar with the subject(s).

I sincerely hope you enjoyed this book. If you did, please comment about it on social media and, surely, write an Amazon or Goodreads review.

And, of course, please tell a friend about this book – especially if your friend owns an RV or is thinking about getting one.

Thank you for your support,

Dale Lee Sumner

p.s. You may want to check out the **RV Blog** page on our website: sumdalus.com

www.ingramcontent.com/pod-product-compliance
Lightning Source LLC
Chambersburg PA
CBHW071313060426
42444CB00034B/2127